Sure, I'll Join Your Cult

Sure, I'll Join Your Cult

A MEMOIR OF MENTAL ILLNESS AND THE QUEST TO BELONG ANYWHERE

MARIA BAMFORD

GALLERY BOOKS
NEW YORK LONDON TORONTO SYDNEY NEW DELHI

G

Gallery Books
An Imprint of Simon & Schuster, Inc.
1230 Avenue of the Americas
New York, NY 10020

Some names and identifying characteristics have been changed.

Internet addresses given in this book were accurate at the time it went to press. The author and publisher are not responsible for changes to third-party websites.

First Gallery Books hardcover edition September 2023

GALLERY BOOKS and colophon are registered trademarks of Simon & Schuster, Inc.

Interior design by Kathryn A. Kenney-Peterson

Manufactured in the United States of America

10 9 8 7 6 5 4 3 2 1

Library of Congress Cataloging-in-Publication Data

Names: Bamford, Maria, author.
Title: Sure, I'll join your cult : a memoir of mental illness and the quest to belong anywhere / Maria Bamford.
Other titles: Sure I will join your cult
Description: First Gallery Books hardcover edition 2023 | New York : Gallery Books, 2023.
Identifiers: LCCN 2023008307 (print) | LCCN 2023008308 (ebook) | ISBN 9781982168568 (hardcover) | ISBN 9781982168582 (ebook)
Subjects: LCSH: Bamford, Maria | Comedians—United States—Biography. | Mentally ill—United States—Biography.
Classification: LCC PN2287.B16355 A3 2023 (print) | LCC PN2287.B16355 (ebook) | DDC 792.702/8092 [B] —dc2/eng/20230522
LC record available at https://lccn.loc.gov/2023008307
LC ebook record available at https://lccn.loc.gov/2023008308

ISBN 978-1-9821-6856-8
ISBN 978-1-9821-6858-2 (ebook)

To all my people (family, friends, twelve-step programs, comedians).

Thank you for not kicking me out. I'll see you at the potluck.

cult (kŭlt) *n.* 1. A social group defined by its unusual philosophical beliefs.

CONTENTS AT A WINCING GLANCE!

CONTENTS

Sure, I'll Join Your Cult

INTRODUCTION

Sure, I'll Join Your Cult

I love being asked to join, so much so that I will say yes to an invitation without knowing exactly what I have agreed to. When I was in my late twenties, a fellow production secretary at Nickelodeon Animation Studio whom I will call "Tina" told me about an event she was attending at the Hollywood Roosevelt hotel and asked me to accompany her. "OF COURSE, TINA!" Tina had been going through some difficulties that involved muffled weeping in the bathroom. I wanted to support and hoped there might be food. (There was not.)

Tina seemed very excited about this whole evening, and when I met her in the five-hundred-seat conference room packed to the gills, it felt like a good way to spend a Tuesday night. A few different speakers got up and talked about how they had once been pathetic and now—thanks to Heartbouncers—they were vigorous and empowered! Awesome! I applauded and whooped! Good for them!

After the speechifying, we were encouraged to stand up and share openly about our personal sorrows (why we were all there that night). Several people stood, verklempt, detailing varying degrees of failure and tragedy in life. As the event was taking place in LA, there was no shortage of people available for dramatic public speaking off the cuff.

I thought, "Great!" I mean, a little irresponsible, because there didn't seem to be any therapeutic professionals available, but what the hell? Everybody seemed hyped and happy. Did I stand up and freestyle prose? No. Not for lack of desire, but I had already been getting all my monologuing out at open mics and twelve-step support groups. And these sad-sack recruits seemed like they had never told anyone anything personal—that, to them, talking to a big group about private issues was a revelatory breakthrough. I thought I'd be generous and "give my time back to the room."

After two hours of Moth workshop–style storytelling and boxes of Kleenex passed, they set us up with a Heartbouncers rep on our own for what I thought might be an unlicensed free coaching sesh.

HEARTBOUNCERS REP: Are you ready to meet your potential?

ME: Yeah!

HR: Let's sign you up for the weekend workshop!

ME: Okay!

HR: We take credit cards or cash!

ME: Oh! I don't have any money! At all!

HR: What are you afraid of?

ME: Fulfilling my potential?

HR: Do you know anyone who might have the money to support you in becoming your best self?

ME: No! No one at all!

I explained to the Heartbouncers rep that I was already in a cult that forbade me from spending money I didn't have (more on that later). I really wanted to go. I did. Who doesn't want to have guaranteed greatness in life for only $1,500 and a weekend at a Courtyard by Marriott in Glendora? The Heartbouncers rep didn't want to let me leave. She pleaded with me not to "self-sabotage" my life like I "always do." I felt for her. It's hard to watch someone make mistakes. I told her gently but sternly it was not her fault what happened to me once I left this ballroom. I gave her both eyeballs to let her know that she'd done her very best to save me from myself.

As I tried to get up and grab my purse to leave, my pal Tina joined in encouraging me to sign up (I believe she got a rebate if one of her marks "hit"). And so I did what I did when escaping many relationships at the time: I got up abruptly and wordlessly ran away. I genuinely—at pace—jog-sprinted out of the hotel back to my 1988 Toyota Corolla I'd parked on the dark streets of Hollywood and drove to a 7-Eleven for a pack of hot peanuts, thereby manifesting several dreams on my vision board at that time in the process. (I love *Runner's World* magazine and always have a few roughly torn-out images of a 10K participant—though I myself have yet to run such a race.)

Even though Heartbouncers didn't take, I am very fond of suddenly adopting a new set of ideals in order to receive welcome from any rigid group of weirdos. If these people wanted a piece of me so badly, I *must* have been okay. (I am *not* okay.)

I have always been drawn to strange and ritualistic groups. In the same way that my mom proselytized about the Bible and the Hilton, I will tell anyone about the already-well-known For Dummies book series—the step-by-step guides filled with graphic icons, cartoons, and easy-to-skim-for-the-info-that-you're-really-looking-for tables of contents. And as tribute I've included some helpful iconography throughout:

ICONOGRAPHY USED IN THIS BOOK

The section following will be in TRIGGER FONT (**Bold Comic Sans**) so you know where the creepy stuff is located. If you don't like me personally, change all fonts in this book with your own pen to **Bold Comic Sans**.

OLD MATERIAL ALERT. Yes, I make some of the same jokes that I have made live onstage, and yes, that is a real letdown. I am also disappointed. Let's feel that together!

ANY BREAKING OF TWELVE-STEP CULT RULES OF ANONYMITY. I'll also try to footnote any backlash from a "higher power" I've received for having revealed publicly my membership in several specific twelve-step groups. Nothing says safe like a secret society!

RECIPES!

FINANCIAL INFORMATION YOU DIDN'T ASK FOR. Sharing the numbers is a part of the money cult (Debtors Anonymous) and goddammit, my compulsive need to overshare is not going to be silenced.

Though I will not label myself "dumb," I'm open to being called a "Dummie™." As I get older, I get much Dummer™—I mumble, I shake, I close my eyes when I speak, trying to remember the definition of words like "dearth." Along with the formatting, I like the For Dummies series because it's a good idea to look up how to do things before you give it a whirl. And from all the mental health Instagram feeds I follow, I note that it is imperative to ask for help (from where this help is to come can be a little more vague).

I have never written a book before. The book you're reading here is the nonfiction equivalent of a stand-up comedian who has done one open mic but will now perform an hourlong comedy special, improvising off drunk crowd suggestions. (It's not going to win a Pulitzer.)

I have *Deep Space Nine* respect for the writers of mental health memoirs. I have read a lot of them. I've read and reread Mary Karr's *Lit,* William Styron's *Darkness Visible,* Elyn Saks's *The Center Cannot Hold,* Kay Redfield Jamison's *Night Falls Fast, Madness* by Marya Hornbacher, and, of course, genius Daniel Smith's masterpiece on anxiety, *Monkey Mind.* (Full disclosure: Daniel Smith is one of the freelance editors I hired to help me with this book, as is Ashley Ray, writer-gorgeous-polyamorous-bisexual-podcaster-comic at www.theashleyray.com.)

In an effort to write this book, I went back to my favorite source for assistance: a used For Dummies title. Or, more specifically, a two-dollar, fairly battered 2018 edition of *Memoir Writing for Dummies.* According to *MWFD,* "a memoir needs an overarching story of the character (oneself) wanting something and everything they do to go about getting it."

What have I wanted?

To be someone else entirely. Someone who loves to live.

How have I gone about getting that?

By participating in CULTS!

And by reading self-help books that (temporarily) "CHANGE MY LIFE"!

I have an ongoing joke with my therapist friend Marketa Velehradska (www.marketavtherapy.com) where I'll announce to her: "Guess what! There's this new book [or article, or podcast, or documentary about Mardi Gras bead factories in China] and it has CHANGED MY LIFE." This is common in LA. Most people here are in the midst of having a product or service CHANGE THEIR LIFE! Have you tried MAGIC WANDS!?? THE ENERGY HEALER IN MANHATTAN BEACH WHO ONLY ACCEPTS ZELLE? Wasp's milk? Having a baby at sixty?

Joining cults and reading self-help books are both symptoms of a kind of desperation. And, in fact, this is an uneven story about one person, specifically a white fifty-two-year-old comic (me/she/her) living in Altadena, California, and how I have kept going when I didn't really want to.

If you have any mentals, you probably know what I mean. I'm not suicidal, but I'm also not particularly psyched. If I've had my first can of Diet Coke plus a nitro cold brew coffee, I get *some* work done. That is, I make my bed. (I didn't make my bed today.) I know, mostly from pro-life billboards, that LIFE IS A GIFT. (And I like to call antiabortion clinics and have them take the time to prove it to me.) Now that I'm on the right meds, I sort of get it. There is something fun about being at a new or old place with or without other people. But I want to err on the conservative side in promoting the magic of gratitude. (An oft-suggested idea by twelve-steppers is to "write a gratitude list," which can be helpful as a reframe, but it's not, etc.)

Bottom line: this is comedic. I do not know what I'm talking about. And full disclaimer: cults, books, books about cults, and comedy are no replacement for meds. Medicine is the best medicine. I'll tell you more about my drug experiences later—of which the last mixture of chemicals has worked out "okay." I don't believe any psychiatric care is optimal—I've had a share of shit, shaming experiences involving mental health treatment from free and expensive institutions. Don't feel bad if you can't find the "right" practitioner or med mix. What I have now is a psychiatric nurse I can text, and his name is Mike. He's pleasant from what I can tell and always refills my scripts within twenty-four hours, which is more than I can say for any psychiatrist I've ever had. The meds I am on make me sleepy and shaky, and my tum-tum is rounder. If it helps to know that a millionaire (my hub and I have three million in assets if you include our house) has not found the best ANYTHING for mentals, know that I am that millionaire.

And in fact, I received this book deal because of my popularity as a comedian. That doesn't mean that you have ever heard of me. I've been performing what I call stand-up for thirty years and I've done a bunch of other stuff. According to my IMDb, 99 percent of it is voice-over. This makes sense, since I am at my most comfortable alone in a chilly booth with soundproof walls between myself and other human beings.

I was told I can't include an entire IMDb listing in my book. I guess it's not what Faulkner meant when he said, "Don't be a 'writer,' but instead be *writing*." So I'll try to explain why one person gets a book deal over another: I had a TV show for two seasons on Netflix, very loosely based on my life. I have acted by acting in acting roles, one of which was Emmy-nominated! I won Best Club Comic at the American Comedy Awards (?) (a money-laundering scheme, as so much of entertainment is). That same year, Bill Cosby was honored as a legend and in a tracksuit lectured the comedians gathered on the importance of Being Funny No Matter What in the humorless, retrospectively aggro manner of an unregistered sex offender. But my professional writing experience, aside from my own stand-up material, consists of two short essays for the *New York Times* and one for *McSweeney's*. Not enough, right?

In my defense—and I am always (adorably?) trying to protect myself—compulsively telling everybody everything may be a big part of the reason I have an audience. As far as I can tell, full disclosure is a CASH COW.

I am like the pathetic stump the grown-up boy sits on at the end of *The Giving Tree*. But instead of a quiet place to rest, I provide you with my splintered, discomfiting need to reveal all my thoughts and flaws—which is either radical honesty or narcissistic showboating. It depends on whom you ask (and don't ask my sister). My husband, Scott, points out that in oversharing, I have sometimes misjudged my audience.*

But if I can be grandstandingly open about something taboo, maybe someone else might feel a little less isolated by knowing my own sad story (and have a few laughs)? And isn't that a useful service to provide? (I ask? Needily?) I have received so much help from others bravely sharing the pariah-ready deets of their lives: Brooke Shields (postpartum intrusive-thought OCD), Naomi Judd (bankruptcy), comedian Richard Lewis (Cookie Monster bulimia—that's the kind of bulimia where you chew your food for a long time . . . and then spit it out. I tried this type of bulimia. It took self-control I do not have. I guess I'm a swallowing gal!).

And speaking of comedians who have yalped out about health issues: Jonathan Winters (now dead) was open about his bipolar diagnosis way back in the 1960s. And then, years later, in the eighties, he was helpful to me! I had just gotten out of the psych ward for the first time. I told everyone I met at the time that "I jez got-oot o da psych wod!" (That's freshly medicated for: "I just got out of the psych ward.") The owner of our local coffee shop, Anja, was upbeat but confused by my new daily greeting (though it may be why she occasionally gives me free coffee). I hadn't found the right medication and felt frighteningly "off." I had a complete loss of confidence in doing anything. Words were . . . Not? Come? To . . . geh??! into sentences properly and my hands tremored like a jackhammer. My friend Dan P. asked me to lunch. I arrived at the cafe and said what I was saying to everyone at the time:

"I jez got-oot o da psych wod!"

---

* I once attempted a joke about eating my boogers (joyfully) and it split the room into part gag reflex, part rage, and so I dropped this hot-button issue from rotation. I hope a booger-eating memoir will be out on the market soon, but I don't have that kind of courage, despite the savory, convenient, and budget-conscious snacking delights in my face that I dig into daily. PLEASE DON'T TELL ANYONE. HA-HA!

Dan said, "Let's call Jonathan WINTERS! Let's call him right now! I'm good friends with Jonathan Winters! He's been to the psych ward! He'll know what to do!"

```
ME: NO, oh, oh no, agh!
```

But Dan was already talking to him and tossed the phone into my two-handed Parkinson's carry.

```
Comedy Legend Jonathan Winters: Hello?
ME: Tenk oo.
CLJW: You're welcome.
ME: I—mnmnm?
CLJW: You got a good shrink?
ME: Uh-humph.
CLJW: Well, then, you just keep going, kid.
ME: Tenk oo vey mush.
```

YOU JUST KEEP GOING, KID. That's great advice!—if not really the only advice you can give anyone under any and all circumstances. And I have kept going. Now I'm writing this book and doing what I do best, which is brazenly going on and on and on about myself. The book is roughly organized with some educational photos and easy recipes that take only a minute of wavering focus. As well as clarifying financial details that will probably only confuse and irritate, but will help me to feel as if I said it ALL, in a scentless, foot-long fecal rope, clearing the bowel.

For example:

💰 This is how much I was paid for doing this book so far and it will be blacked out on being published but just ask me and I'll tell you in person:

Three years ago, I was given $XK to start.

I gave that entire $XK to editors to help me along the way because I cannot do things without someone watching me like a hawk.

If this book ever gets published—and we don't know if it will—I will get another $XK.

And if the book ever gets made into a softcover, I will get another $XK.

My takeaway—after taxes, commissions, and editorial costs—will amount to about $XK over the course of six years. Good to know! (I did not quit my day job as a comedian.)

Full disclosure: THIS book is NOT going to have a clear chronicle of trauma, healing, victory. It's going to be more like a series of emotional sudoku puzzles that I grow tired of trying to solve and a third of the way through start a new one, hoping the next one is easier. I haven't figured it out. I don't relate well to stories where people have found some sparkling new reality at the end of the memoir. Sometimes memoirists have to write a second memoir to amend their initial new reality to a new, NEW reality of what's now really real for them. And I am NOT writing a second book. Unless of course anyone at all offers me money.

RIGOROUS HONESTY ABOUT LYING

Whenever someone gets caught for saying they were on the seventieth floor of the World Trade Center on September 11 when in fact they were returning a blouse at Strawberry in Midtown, I always feel compassion and a twinge of anxiety. I punch up history. Or rather, I describe events and then add "elements" to make the narrative pop. This is called lying like a Ruggable.

I want to place blame on my mother, who always had very polite workarounds (fabrications) she told over the phone for not doing things at church (a place where you're not supposed to do a lot of lying).

MARILYN: [*dramatic sigh*] Listen, I'm sorry. We just can't. We already have a "dinner" that night. And it's just crazy with Halloween coming up because Maria wants to go as an eel. [That dinner consisted of frozen fish sticks around the glowing TV with my mother eating a tart Granny Smith sliced in fourteen pieces while on the phone with her pal Maren Hustad, and I was going to Halloween as I always do, as a "jogger."]

My sister also adds a bit of zing to reality: "Then I said to the waiter, 'We're not vegan, we're just weird!' And he gave US a tip!" Her husband, Mark, will sometimes almost inaudibly interrupt her stories with, "That didn't happen." Oh well. I was riveted!

This tendency to punch up the truth may also come from Bamford family dinners. In order to get the attention of a crowd of three Bamfords in the '70s/'80s, you had to close big. And if you're the youngest and are not having a lot of life experiences, forget holding court. My sister headlined most meals, with my mom as the gregarious emcee, and my dad featured with Dr. Pimple Popper–style derm stories of explosive boils and phantom itches. I was allowed a short guest set. My dad would set the egg timer for three minutes—like any good showroom runner—and that's when I got more than a hundred seconds to grab my audience with some fifth-grade perspectives. Dinosaur graves, volcanic ash, boys who hit me—I kept it tight. I would get to speak without outside comment for three glorious minutes—preparing me for later episodes of Byron Allen's *Comics Unleashed*, which was like doing stand-up in a support-group-like setting sitting down and STILL PAYS ME GENEROUS RESIDUALS. Byron Allen is a comic's friend as well as a billionaire. Much respect.

This storytelling technique of adding things in and removing parts can be called "craft" or, if you're a stickler/lawyer/good person, trickery, false testimony, perjury. In performance, I like to recount the story of my mom visiting her oncologist for the last time, right after surviving a deadly pleural effusion and deciding on hospice. Leaving the appointment, she said joyfully: "I lost four pounds!!"

Did I leave out some parts of the conversation? Yes. One of the reasons she wanted to stop treatment was because of being puffed up with IV fluids. When my mom said, "I lost four pounds!" she was also celebrating being out of the hospital and not uncomfortably swelled up with water and attached to machines. You might say, *Well, that makes it different. She just wanted to feel more comfortable.* Yes, you're right. I should be stopped.

But, look, there is truth that my mom has always been weight-focused and she did express satisfaction about reaching goal weight in the year before she died. I DID tell her that even if a coffin is tight around the hips, eventually it fits! She told me not to use that in my act. But the joke's on me: She got herself cremated and now she's just a POUND! She can wear ANYTHING!

Here's another close-to-truth-yet-still-a-lie lie. In a joke, I say that I have tried to commit suicide. And it is true that I did, when I was ten years old, ingest a bottle of Tums in order to cause damage. (All that happened was I got sent to Christian therapy and had good bone growth.) So it's true, but it's laughable. And in more recent years, I have hoarded meds and looked up ways to die painlessly on Google. But have I made a serious attempt? No. Have I ever put a razor to my wrist lengthwise in the bathtub? No, but again, as a ten-year-old—I DID slather my lower arms with ketchup and lie in the front hall of the house with a butter knife in my hand until my parents found me and asked me to take a shower and shampoo the residual tomato paste product out of the carpet.

I'm not sure how much of this anxiety about what the truth is comes from my OCD scrupulosity and what is related to the actual standards of journalism, but just take everything I say with three to one thousand grains of pink Himalayan sea salt.

HOW TO USE THIS BOOK

This is not doctrine. Disagree from the margins in jumbo Sharpie. Flick through each page with maple syrup and artificial spray butter on your fingers. Skip ahead to the last page to leave a full, sticky handprint. Tear off pages, yell out in refusal while skimming. DO NOT READ THE WHOLE THING. I certainly haven't. Take in the parts that interest you—the verbs, the spooky photos, the stirring numbers. Memorize only this page inside your local independent bookstore while sitting on the floor. Put it back in the sports section and buy *Shoe Dog* by Phil Knight instead. Then, quickly trade *Shoe Dog* for the trashed Gideon Bible in the Little Free Library right outside of the bookstore. Next, toss God's Word in your backyard compost heap. Remember how much you like podcasts.

BEYOND THIS BOOK

You've done more than enough.

WHERE TO GO FROM HERE

Fall asleep face-first in a plated Slurpee, drift off into unconsciousness, follow your feelgood (™ my sister, life coach, and shaman, Sarah Bamford Seidelmann, www.followyourfeelgood.com).

PART I

My Indoctrination: The Cult of Family

1. Getting Current: What Life Is Like Now

Just so you know I mean it when I say that things are not at all on their way to perfect, I will describe for you a recent day that my husband and I had together. We are still developing a mission statement, business plan, and uniform for our cult of two. It seems to be: "CHUNK!," $1,500 a month on Grubhub for pizza/taco parties, and handmade puffy-paint T-shirts.

And calm yourself: We are still alive at the end of this story. And we are getting tons of outside twelve-step cult help (Recovering Couples Anonymous! as well as individual therapy, couples therapy, and psychiatry).

It's Thursday, and Scott and I get up at 11 a.m. Our daily schedule includes ten hours of sleep and a two-hour afternoon nap. It is also the middle of the Covid pandemic so there may be some light depression keeping us affixed to our California king–size mattress. I like a lack of structure, but Covid has been a lot of sloshing around. I have this list of goals posted in my closet:

2020
BELONGING
I'M AT
HOME IN
THE WORLD

make copy of all records & have in car.

Spirit
I Do enough
I have enough
I am enough
Meditate 2x a day
walk an hour a day and talk to myself.
write down numbers end of day.
one ... position

Emotional
work step 1 w/ Al-Anon sponsor
work step 4 w/ DA sponsor.
Keep Mon/Tues sacred - see what happens.
Take a college class towards a masters

Financial
- Take 24 hours before any purchase or transactions over $500 and call 3 people
- Give 11% of Net Biz income to charity, imperfectly.

Community
- Go to a community meeting for Altadena
- Say "Hello" boisterously to every Neighbor.

Self-care
brush & floss 1x a day
hair blown out 1x/week.

Relationships:
See therapists every week.
Treat Scott like a hotel guest and beloved relative
Every day call 3 frieds and ask how they are?

Creativity
1-10 minute crowd work set a week.
Write about process of new hour 10-minute/day.
cowork. every week w/ a fried.
volunteer to help others.

Business
Youtube channel completed + uploaded.
- speak w/ co-workers on the phone + ask them how they are
- send a thank you note once a week.
- take the time w/ categorizing Income/expenses.
- complete a business pl...

Home
- Firepla...
- Neighborhood pa... party.
- 20 min... day or chore
- make th... bed
de-clutter every day

Did it go through the wash? Yes. Do I actually do this stuff? Of course not. This is from 2020. I forgot about this list posted in the closet for a whole year. I made this list after a 9.6-ounce can of Starbucks nitro cold brew with a mini cappuccino Clif Bar chaser. I was cracked!

Back to Thursday: I'm irritable. I haven't exercised in a few days, so I feel "fat," which I understand to be a part of my 1980s white-woman heritage. It is stupid and useless, as "fat," of course, is not a feeling. It isn't conversation, as my dear friend and barn-burning powerhouse of comedy Jackie Kashian (of *Conan*, HBO's *2 Dope Queens*, the *Jackie and*

Laurie Show podcast, and the *Dork Forest* podcast) says. And I am not fat. I am norm on the low side. I am five foot six and 133 pounds. What I may be feeling is "fail." My Debtors Anonymous sponsor, Bernice, just dumped me. I was working the steps of Debtors Anonymous on time management.

I seem to have a polychronic understanding of time based on relationships and the tides that really bums out my manager, the great Bruce Smith. I call him, running late on a weekly basis on days when I only have ONE JOB THAT DAY. So, with Bernice, as you might predict, I screwed up and missed several scheduled calls. It is because I can't stop being late or confusing times in my work and personal life that I was trying to change via "step work." (The steps, FYI, are kind of like a Catholic confession but with peer support, hazy spiritual-type language, behavior modification, and understanding laffs.) After I missed the third appointment we had made, Bernice decided that my admitted poor time management not only wasted her time but also hurt her feelings. Therefore, a seventy-five-year-old Glendale woman who had spent several hours of her final years on earth listening to me and my bunk was compelled to break up with me by text.

> Hi Maria—I'm not able to continue with step work nor to schedule calls or PRGs [Pressure Relief Groups]—always happy to receive outreach calls and will respond as I can. As always, all the best with your book and all else!

EEWWW-NEEEEW. I was (embarrassingly) surprised, as I hadn't totally realized how much my flakiness affected people. I apologized for my inexcusable conduct. And then I asked Bernice—just for clarity, so I could confirm it was me being an asshole—what was the reason she would no longer be available. It's important to be interested in why people are done with you! (And it's also okay if they don't answer. At that point, leave people you've hurt ALONE.) But Bernice kindly responded:

> Maria!! So nice to hear from you! You were/are lovely—I just felt like there were one too many times I went out of my way to make myself available, rearrange my schedule, etc., and then for whatever reason you couldn't show up. Or you'd call, I'd interrupt my work to call back immediately, and you wouldn't pick up. So just a dif way of communicating. When we met for step work you were always super prompt and prepared and respectful of my time and the work, which I so appreciated! I hope our paths cross again and I am always here if you want to chat—hope you and Scott are well and Happy Thanksgiving 🐿️🍂

So there you have it, complete with seasonal emoticons: I am a real asswipe. I now have a new Debtors Anonymous sponsor, Dez, with whom I was totally up-front about the noise I pulled with Bernice, and I am now limiting myself to just calling Dez "in the moment." With no plans or expectations for return calls. Like a drunk with a calendar, I can't seem to handle having one appointment, like a lady. Now, back to our loving couple:

Scott and I drive to Café de Leche. I am, as I said, feeling angry at myself. We get very strong coffee. We walk to the park near the cafe to find a Covid-safe outdoors spot where we can sit, but the Mexican restaurant next door is blasting one song, "Feliz Navidad," over and over and over again to discourage people from loitering, even though that is exactly what parks are for: to loiter in. I understand that they don't want the unhoused good people of Los Angeles to dwell and drop guano in the park, but LA doesn't have many places for unhoused people to dwell and drop guano—and what better place to dwell and drop than a park?

Just know that this part of the story may be creepy to people who have had mentals or thought the way I do, and I will list the suicide hotline at the end like a responsible mental health advocate, even though I myself find that precaution to be slightly condescending. Don't we all know what the fucking number is at this point? I'm depressed, I'm not a moron. TEXT "HOME" TO 741741. Or dial 988.

STOP **We walk back to the car in an effort to go to the other nearby park with less stereo. I think at this point, Scott would agree he's on edge—for reasons of his own that may have to do with being on the mood-disorder spectrum. Scott is driving. He makes a sharp turn up the hill to the other park. He asks me to look for the OTHER park on my phone. And because I think I know where the park is from memory, I don't look for the park on my phone. I am looking at my phone, but I am watching a video. With the sudden movement uphill, I accidentally dump my coffee in my lap and onto the seat of our new-to-us 2015 Toyota RAV4 Hybrid. I make a noise that sounds like "owp." It's a big mess. I start to cry. Scott is pissed because instead of looking for the park, I had been watching a video on Instagram of a rescued beaver who makes dams of decorative pillows in his new suburban home.**

Scott is too upset to continue with the Second Park Plan. He three-point pivots our fully stained vehicle back to our house. When we arrive home, he closes himself in the garage studio and listens to records. I go back to my office, sob-heaving to myself, staring out a window, as I have thousands of times since the age of nine, and dredge up all of the things that, in my mind, make me an unwanted person. My friends don't like me. My family hates me. I'm somehow responsible for the death of my mother, or at least for the fact that she suffered. I'm untrustworthy. I'm self-centered. A seventy-five-year-old writer and Debtors Anonymous sponsor hath

forsook me. I focus on whatever confirms that I *should* be crying and that it's really best if I'm obliterated. I once told a fellow comic about this hobby of longing for death and they said, "Why don't you just do it?" Comedians can be like that. "Kill myself, you mean?" And yes, because the comedian is a skilled jokesmith, that is exactly what they mean. Ha-ha! I see what they are getting at. They're tired of hearing about this project and they just want me to Make It Happen! But, unfortunately (?), suicidal urges have always been more like fantasy football to me, an avocation done on weekends.

Feeling sorry for myself, I then take out my laptop to google the medications I have in the house plus "overdose." According to Google, none of the medications I have are supereffective in suicide attempts. All of the medical journal entries I read are about how they quickly were able to save the patient from these kinds of ODs. After a few minutes of halfhearted, haphazard research, I don't take action toward harming myself.

What I do instead is I cry and cry and cry and cry and then go make a Guy Fieri–size sandwich with a Sara Lee everything bagel, turkey, cheese, and veganaise. I eat it in bed while reading the *New York Times Book Review* and I fall asleep covered in preserved crumbs. When I wake up, Scott is sitting by the pool. Yes, we have a pool. And we both are dreaming of our demise. Nobody wants to hear it. As my hysterically funny friend Jackie Kashian put it, "You can only complain laterally," or, don't go on and on about your mental illness while also mentioning your pool. If it helps you feel less resentful, the pool isn't heated and is filled with dying bees, pine needles, and stinging ants. I have also peed in it several times over the three years we've lived here, and now you are one of the few people who knows that besides every other person I've told.

From an LA smog- and grime-covered gray plastic lounge seat, Scott makes a grackle noise that we use to cry out to each other from different ends of our seventy-year-old ranch home filled with spiders (and, as we will soon find out, RATS! They will thunder inside the walls of our home for years before we can pay to have them relocated).

"AAAA . . . AACK," he says.

"AAAAA . . . AACK," I respond.

We apologize to each other—Scott for getting so upset and not going to the park, me for being on my phone and not helping us get to the park. And because we're supposed to tell each other this stuff, I own up about my googling OD instructions.

Scott responds, "Yeah, me too. I thought about borrowing one of Mike's guns. You should have asked me about how to OD. You just drink alcohol with Xanax. We have both."

And we laugh. I had totally forgotten about the Xanax! Hahaha! A handshake agreement is made that—at least for today—neither of us will kill ourself. (Don't worry! We have a safety-plan agreement we got from the National Suicide Prevention Hotline clamped in a magnetic Chip Clip and hung on our refrigerator, witnessed and notarized by Carol Grisham, MFT, of Pasadena, California, who takes all insurance but may retire soon. So make your appointments NOW.) And FYI, I'm not a real candidate for suicide: statistically, it's people who've had one real attempt, mostly men—which, as I write this, I realize is the exact description of Scott.

The story above might not bode well for us. It is quite possibly very, very bad. I know that. Scott knows that. The Grish, our therapist (Carol

Grisham, MFT, Pasadena), knows that. But many times, due to my own actions, personality, diagnosis—whatever you want to call it—things have not been "all good."

But feeling ashamed and not telling anyone about it has NEVER HELPED. My hope is that by telling people about all this stuff, maybe others will relate. And then I won't feel alone? And yes, of course, I'll call my psychiatric nurse, Matt. Though he just changed insurances and I need to find somebody else. And Scott will call his therapist and his psychiatrist. And yes, we will call Deda and Jim from our Recovering Couples Anonymous meeting we've been attending and they will laugh. Deda will say, "Are you trying to scare each other?" Yes, yes we are! We thought it might help! And yes, twelve-steppers, we are "WORKING THE STEPS of the program," you sanctimonious church basement carps! We are on step four, if you must know.

I'd like to blame the above morning episode on myself or my poor diet or the city of Los Angeles or something about how and who I am that might be solved, but let's just call it a Thursday.

FREE COFFEE

1. Get to know every single barista/o in your local coffee shop. That's Emma, Jason, Helen, Anjara, Brooklyn, and Jeremy! And because there's high turnover, now it's Angela, Jeremiah, Lupe, Jason, and Carmela! Oops—now Amber, Kat, Jonny, and Jason! Learn the names of their pets. Ask about their cat, Stanley. Like and repost their self-made music videos of ballet dancing while high. Give them your address and the code to get into your house to use the pool.
2. After two to seven months of this, forget to pay. That's twelve ounces of your favorite coffee beverage gratis!
3. Become CONSUMED WITH GUILT. You just STOLE five-dollars-plus out of the pocket of a small, family-owned business in your own neighborhood! Anja, the owner, will find out and you will be BANNED.
4. Within twenty-four hours, send ten dollars via Venmo to Anja.
5. REPEAT THIS PROCESS FOR DECADES.

2. Diagnos-YES!

Why I need so badly to belong somewhere:
because there's something really wrong with me!

STOP Somewhere between nine and eleven years old—I'm terrible with dates—after many sleepless nights, I pad-pad-padded in my Lanz flannel nightgown down to my parents' bedroom. My dad must have been in his study, because I remember only my mom there, in her Protestant white linen nightgown that she would wear to bed. She sat reading in bed with her legs bent-splayed, with no underwear. BLECH. You couldn't see anything, but just knowing was enough for me to feel very anxsh. That is because for the past year—as a nine-to-eleven-year-old—I had been tormented by the obsession and fear that I was a violent sexual-deviant-molester-genocidal-monster disguised as a sixth grader with a lopsided dimple and a Dorothy Hamill haircut. I hadn't slept for months. It is hard to lose consciousness when you're clenching your face and fists to prevent yourself from killing your family. I don't know why police have never told sociopaths that you can wince and sit on your hands in order to physically prevent yourself from mayhem. Anyhoo, I wasn't feeling well. I was beginning to pull away from my family (and friends) out of a fear that I would tit-touch-knife them. The only relief was suicidal ideation. But that night, I dared to tell my mom a smidge of what had been going on in my head.

How did this intrusive-thought OCD start? It was around the same time my sister started giving me titty twisters and calling me a freak. In response to this treatment, I feared I was going to grab at my sister or give her a titty twister in return. Then I started feeling ANXSH that I was going to give my *mother* a titty twister. The unwanted image would pop into my brain and I'd feel sick and scared. I'd try to get the distressing idea to go away, which as anyone who has ever tried not to think of something (gel pens, your ex's lack of internet presence, emu farming) knows, it only made me think about it more. Before long, these repetitive obsessive cringes developed into the revulsion that I would attack and twist and slice off or lick or otherwise molest the boobs of my sister and my mother or any other female I encountered. Then I'd clench my fists and my face to make the thoughts go away, but the alarming visions kept coming. Over and over again, all day, every day, I'd sit on my hands and tightly squeeze my nine-to-eleven-year-old fists and flat little butt cheeks. Through this method, I disabled my tiny arms from mammary-maiming every chesty cunt in my eyeline.

How far did these thoughts go? The answer is: not very. Nothing really happens beyond the undesired, offensive slideshow in my own mind. There's the obsession with the unwanted thought, and then the compulsion or ritualized behavior, which (momentarily) stops the obsession. For example, you pass an old man on the street and for whatever reason you notice his butt. If you're normal, you just think, "Oh, that was a butt. A boo-tay." And you go on to your next thought that involves your own butt or your job title or what kind of car you'd drive off a cliff. But if you have OCD, after "BUTT THOUGHT" you think something along the lines of, "OH CHRIST! I SAW A PERSON AND THEN I THOUGHT OF THEIR BUTT AND THAT'S REALLY WRONG!!!!! I MUST NOT EVER THINK THAT THOUGHT AGAIN! NO BUTTS! NO BUTTS!"

You now can't stop thinking about the idea that you thought of someone's butt, and so the butt thought keeps coming back, as does the thought that you *shouldn't* be thinking about butts and trying to rid your brain of old-man-butt thoughts. The compulsion is whatever you do to try to get the thought out of your head—so that can be avoidance (of butts or old men with butts), or rituals you make up, like, "I'll walk a hundred steps backward and that will make the butt thought 'neutral'" (whereupon the butt thought comes up again and you've got to take another hundred steps backward). Which for a while might actually be fun until you trip and fall back on your own butt.

I'd stop the thoughts by avoiding human interaction as much as possible. If it was unavoidable, I would do a combo stomach crunch/buttock pinch, hoping no one would "see" the ghastly *Guernica* inside my head.

But after about a year of this with no letup, I told my mom.

I didn't say, succinctly, "I'm worried I'm going to hack and chop off your 32Bs and then put my little fifth-grade hand up your tweedledee," or, "I can't let you or Sarah touch me because then I'd lose control and behead and suckle your pink tiddlywinks and wedge your furry horse hoof." In that case, I'm sure she would have freaked out a bit more. I was a tad more vague.

"Mom. I can't sleep. I'm afraid I'm going to hurt everyone at night."

My mom was a type A stay-at-home mom. In addition to caring for the two of us, she was extremely well-coiffed and belonged to two book groups, something called a "birthday" group (where you have monthly lunches for ongoing birthdays), and a Bible-study group. At the same time, she was attending grad school for a social-work degree, was a deacon in the church, volunteered at a women's domestic violence center, and kept our house looking like the Westin, with lots of pure white linens at the ready. She had a slew of friends, a full dance card, and a lifetime membership at WeightWatchers.

All of which is to say, by the time I got to her bedroom that night, Marilyn had probably downed a couple of pots of coffee and run out of calories for the day. Although typically empathetic to any new problem brought to her by the family's Resident Weeper (me), she probably wasn't operating on all cylinders when she responded to my concerns:

"Oh, honey, it's okay if you're gay."

It was 1980. I was nine to eleven years old. I wasn't clear what being gay meant. But I assumed it was worse than being a matri-sporicidal de-breasting pedo-maniacal pervert. She sounded a little freaked out, but it could have been the dehydration caused by her abuse of sugar-free chocolate Alba shakes.

"It's okay. Go back to bed," she said.

I went back to bed. And because I was the crier of my family, I cried. At first, I felt some lightness from finally having told someone about the oddball things I'd been thinking—thoughts I coded in my red plaid quilted diary under "The Fears." At least I had tried. Then I cried in a way that I have done many times since, filled with self-pity and yearning for unconsciousness. I thought that I must be an unfathomable outlier (as we all thought we were prior to the internet). I probably shouldn't tell anyone else about these fearful thoughts again if I wanted to continue being invited to be a member of society. And I didn't tell anyone. Until I was thirty-five. And now again, at fifty-two, in this book!

DO YOU HAVE OCD? Questionnaire by Maria B.

Some signs you have intrusive-thought OCD. FYI, these thoughts are often the worst thing you can possibly think of happening. For me, in the 1980s, that meant "What if I'm gay because I have friends who are girls?" Let the zeitgeist or your surrounding culture's taboos guide you. The following are funnier versions—though if you actually have intrusive thoughts, they feel paralyzing and personal. I in no way want to suggest they are "fun," but they can be "funny."

- ❑ Are you concerned that, despite not having the desire to access a katana, you will eviscerate me, Maria Bamford, with a katana?
- ❑ Are you worried that you have driven over someone's body (earlier today)? Do you want to go check? I'll stay here. Go check! And after you check, check again!
- ❑ Are you somewhat certain that no one is safe around you and the more safe you try to make everything, the less safe things will get? BE SAFE! (Right?)
- ❑ Do you fear having the *thought* that you despise me inherently and that I will know that you hate me? Do you fear that if we ever meet in person, I will know that you think I'm a honky-cracker-bitch-Karen-slut-whore-cunt-ass-whitey-fuck-chop? And that because you even have the thought means that you *really think* I'm honky-cracker-bitch-Karen-slut-whore-cunt-ass-whitey-fuck-chop and so you avoid me at all costs and anyone who looks like me to prevent yourself from acting on your undesired but inherent evil opinions about me that you have but don't have at all?
- ❑ If I were your three-month-old baby—AND I AM NOT—would you avoid spending time with me because you're anxious that you might rip me up into pieces like pull-apart cinnamon monkey bread, then butter and microwave me? Despite the fact that you do NOT have a microwave and you LOVE ME? I am your three-month-old baby! (I am not.)

- ❑ If you're a gay woman lesbian and not a liar, are you a little nervous that maybe you trick everyone all the time—especially about being a gay woman lesbian—and that maybe you're secretly attracted to peen, poles, and dingles? Do you try to avoid talking to males because all you can think about is their testicular beards and pendulous fat hogs you've never seen up close? And you don't think you're attracted to men, but you've eaten a TON of bananas and you won't date and have a committed relationship with a woman until you're SURE you're a *gay woman lesbian*?
- ❑ Do you ever say the words "blessed Jesus Mohammed Yahweh Oprah" three times while squeezing your buttocks to stop yourself from driving your Harley into a grunt of senior citizens?
- ❑ Is it hard to make eye contact with me because you are concerned that you poisoned my liver with your high five? Did you roofie my Diet Coke with arsenic and then forget about it?
- ❑ Do you have your wife get the ice cubes for your drink so that you won't stuff hundreds of ice cubes down your throat, being the first person to self-suicide by drowning, upright, on land?
- ❑ Do you never drink iced tea because "t" stands for "titties" that you're concerned you're going to reach out and touch on the server with titties who brought you tea (which stands for "titties")?
- ❑ Do you ever check with friends after an evening out—whether you've killed them?
- ❑ Again, let's say I'm your baby. Now I'm six months old, but you're still a little scared—despite never having wanted to hurt me or taking an action toward hurting me, you're uncertain

because of the monkey bread idea coming into your head—and in order to avoid causing me any bodily harm, you wear a used Sonic the Hedgehog mascot suit all day and have hired a twenty-four-hour security guard to watch your hands?

- ❑ Have you ever really not wanted to think your mom or dad is "the one"—and so you spend your life playing Candy Crush with friends from Azerbaijan, never leaving your bed so that you don't send romantic mixed signals to one or both of your parents?
- ❑ Have you ever wanted to prove—once and for all—to your partner of ten years, whom you love, that you really, really, *really* love them and that it's really real by getting a tattoo of their face on your face and even after getting it done realized you should have full sleeves of their arm hair on top of your arms or it doesn't "count" and your relationship is DOOMED?
- ❑ If I were a thirteen-year-old pug named Richard—AND I'M NOT—would you look at my photo on Instagram and fearfully gauge for any impromptu sensations in your genitals to make sure you were safe to adopt me despite the fact that *you don't like pugs in that way*?
- ❑ Are you ever terrified that you're cheating on your spouse by drinking boba alone?
- ❑ Do you give twenty-five dollars to charity every time a flash of the Hindu god Ganesh comes to mind (but he's nude and giving you the finger) and you've now donated over 120 thousand dollars to Amnesty International?
- ❑ Have you avoided attending bat and bar mitzvahs out of concern that you're going to run up, grab the Torah, rip off your yarmulke, and start reciting the lyrics of the Wu-Tang Clan song "Bring da Ruckus" (Bring da motherfuckin' ruckus)?

- ❑ Do you repeat under your breath, "Live, love, laugh!" while clutching the "right" purple crystal and running around the mall eleven times to prevent yourself from going to hell (which BTW is DT Fresno at 2 p.m., midsummer)?
- ❑ Do you feel terrified that the Lord God who is RuPaul will know your real thoughts that you have had about *Drag Race*? That you've had really awful thoughts about every contestant and episode, and that because you have had all of these weird thoughts, our Lord and Savior Father Mother God RuPaul will smite you—perhaps right, right now? With a sudden aneurysm that you will be fully conscious of and that is happening as you read this and so you need to tweet RuPaul hashtags of #PraiseWithoutCeasing? And that because of this responsibility, you can't really devote yourself to working PT for Instacart?
- ❑ Are you doing jumping jacks to prevent ME from exploding? (Uh-oh! I'm exploding anyway!!!! KABLAM!!!!)

AND HERE IN ALL CAPS IS MY OWN OCD "GUARANTEE" MAKING CERTAIN THAT YOU KNOW THAT I'M SAFE—TOLD TO YOU BY A PROFESSIONAL OCD THERAPIST WHO IS REAL.

Dear reader:

I have been friends with Maria Bamford for close to twenty years. Through the years, Maria has often openly shared her experiences with OCD with me. She discussed her struggle with a variety of obsessive thoughts and subsequent compulsive behaviors meant to prevent the distress stemming from these thoughts. Maria shared that she had been experiencing symptoms of OCD from early childhood and through the years experienced several types of OCD including harm, pedophilia (fear of), scrupulosity, and sexual identity, which are all common types of intrusive thoughts.

Maria had been also experiencing intrusive thoughts and anxiety about being racist and transphobic and had generally been worried about being a bad person, which is a typical fear often underlying OCD. Maria's experience with OCD is a common one. Per the National Institute of Mental Health, an estimated 1.2 percent of US adults had OCD in a fairly recent year, yet it's still often misunderstood and misdiagnosed and therefore very difficult to talk about openly even in clinical settings.

Through our friendship, Maria has always been a caring friend with a deep appreciation and love for her family, friends, and community as well as for her four-legged pals. There has never been doubt in my mind that Maria's obsessive thoughts have been anything other than a tormenting symptom of common mental health disorder *[my emphasis].*

Thanks,
Marketa Velehradska, LCSW

RECIPE FOR CHIP OFF THE FLOOR

1. There's a corn chip on the floor! Somebody must have dropped it.
2. Pick it up. It is now yours.
3. Pop it in your mouth.
4. Savor and delight in the chip.
5. EAT IT OPENLY. This is a gift from an exciting and mysterious universe. You are its Minor God.

3. My First Cult: My Family

As the title of this book suggests, I love groups. I love social orders that I can push against while still being held by snug boundaries of membership. Like a baby defecating securely in a diaper. I treasure organizations (in their softer forms). If they're not so unbending that I'm thrown out, then I am allowed to be a contradictory pain in the ass. I want belonging in a thing, but I won't want any of the responsibilities inherent in claiming association. I never worry I'll be a fascist because of ongoing resistance to "pitching in."

THE GURU: MY MOM!

If our family was a cult and we had a leader, our leader was my mom, Marilyn. She was beloved and charismatic, and inspired intense devotion. Back in 2020, I went to Duluth, Minnesota, for a three-month visit to be with Mother Bamford in her final days on earth. I was fifty-one and finally on the right meds, so it was like getting a second chance at growing up in beautiful northern Minnesota, one in which I had a brain that functions. My mom, despite being an oracle, was dying.

A metastasized tumor growing in her lung was pressing on her aortic blood vessel, so she was coughing up blood occasionally. She was in her bed at St. Mary's Medical Center in downtown Duluth, chatting spryly about the DNR (do not resuscitate) order she was about to sign. My mom may have been sick, but she had not lost all of her powers. My mom is a master of getting to know strangers seemingly instantaneously. She can squeeze joy out of a customer-service call.

Typically, by the time she gets off the phone with AT&T, three hours have passed and she has made a rich and joyful connection with a twenty-eight-year-old Black man in an Atlanta call center. Or a young

Brazilian woman in a São Paulo call center. Or a Sikh man in a Mumbai call center. Or a white evangelical lady—"but not the bad kind; she had a sense of humor about herself. A *fun* Baptist"—in a Michigan call center.

A nurse came into Mom's room and in less than five minutes, my mother had amassed the following info about Ellie the nurse:

- Before becoming a nurse, Ellie worked for ten years as an accounting director in Seattle. Ellie did NOT enjoy being an accounting director.
- However, Ellie loved rescuing animals and would spend all her free time caring for diabetic cats and disabled dogs.
- Ellie met a drummer from Duluth.
- Ellie realized that her "bliss" was caring for others.
- Upon coming to this realization, Ellie quit her lucrative accounting job and the very next day applied to nursing school.
- The first job Ellie applied for (this one) was the one she got, and now she is in Duluth with her Duluthian drummer hub.
- Her husband is an excellent drummer but doesn't know the Duluth band Low (which was fronted by Alan Sparhawk and his much-mourned wife, Mimi Parker), nor is he familiar with the Duluth-based singer-songwriter and disability-rights activist Gaelynn Lea, who won NPR's Tiny Desk Contest in 2016.
- Ellie's husband is having a hard time finding musicians to play with in Duluth.
- Ellie's nursing mentor is my mom's neighbor and a fellow Episcopalian who made us really good lasagna the other night.

THIS IS WITHIN LESS THAN FIVE MINUTES.

I recently had to make a customer-service call to hotels.com and attempted to pull a Marilyn. Although a constant traveler, I don't always pick up on the cues that I might be staying in a flophouse. I also take pride in staying anywhere I am put. I never complain or send anything back. I will eat ANYTHING. I will stay ANYWHERE. I WILL COMPLAIN TO NO ONE, much less the underpaid employee in front of me. (Except my own manager, Bruce. I ask Bruce for a lot. Actually, SHOUT-OUT TO BRUCE! SORRY I'M LATE WITH THIS BOOK!)

I reserved Scott and me a room at a Days Inn in Duluth that's right on the freeway. I got there first; Scott was arriving a week later. I didn't want us to stress my mom and dad by taking up their basement, sleeping till noon, and eating all of my dad's Fig Newtons.

DAD: You found my supply!

ME [*covered in crumbs*]: Please, Papa, forgive me.

An inexpensive chain motel/flophouse known to all road comics is a two-star way station. It looks like a hotel—there are towels, beds, cable!

But here are the things that I didn't notice for the seven days I was there before Scott arrived:

- Sopping-wet carpet (I figured it had just been washed—it's the cleanest!)
- Strong smell of mold and cigarette smoke
- Woman next door vomiting all day and night and crying out, "It will never end!" (She had a friend in the room with her trying to help. I had just assumed she was going through something and put in earplugs.)

- Man on other side, getting daily visits from a social worker bringing groceries and court updates. (I thought he was getting Grubhub.)

Scott arrived and noticed all of this within fifteen minutes. Because we have the cash, at Scott's request, I moved us to a quiet Airbnb and I attempted a Marilyn as we left the wet, moldy crisis center also known as the Days Inn.

The young, uncombed concierge at the front desk told me, "Yeah, uh, you have to call the 1-800 number, but um, they probably won't give you a refund because you bought the room in advance." Oh. We're fucked. I see. I said, "Thank you," and did as the young roustabout suggested.

I called hotels.com.

I asked David from hotels.com where he was from (San Salvador, El Salvador). I attempted Spanish but couldn't make it past greetings. In English, I thanked him for his time, verbally bowing with solicitous apologies for his troubles. Unhelpfully, I told him I had been to Honduras once. After this building of goodwill, I explained—not angrily but in a lovingly descriptive way—our unique experiences at the Days Inn. The light flooding, the disturbing noises, the ennui. David was gracious. He sadly notified me (as foretold by the bedhead concierge) that he wouldn't be able to do anything because the room was prepurchased. I expressed gratitude: "I appreciate you even trying, David. I can't even imagine how hard your job is." And it's true. I cannot. I got fired within two hours of having a call-center job.

Subsequently, David put me on hold for about thirteen whole minutes. And then he RETURNED! Whereupon David in El Salvador gave us a FULL REFUND FOR THE REMAINDER OF OUR BOOKING. I will never attain my mother's grace, but I did get $1,100 back from hotels .com, which, from what I understand, is a MIRACLE.

Even still, I could never out-Marilyn Marilyn. My mom was in the hospital again after several trips to the ER. She had a fever, atrial fibrillation, and pain in her esophagus. She was actively dying. A young nurse in training was having trouble getting her blood pressure and my mom cheerfully said, "I'm so glad I'm here to help someone learn!" She curiously asked every nurse where they had gone to nursing school and how they thought the school they went to compared with other local schools. She got the names of their children, the cities the children had moved to, and what jobs they now held.

If my mom exuded healing warmth, I am a cold stone. In those last months, I tried to observe my mother's every move and transform myself into one of the happiest, most socially engaged people I have ever known. (I've got the voice impersonation down, but that's it.)

My mom wasn't perfect. She liked her girls to shine. She was not totally pumped that I'd taken three months away from LA to come to Duluth. For her death. On her brand-new, free hospice deathbed (TREAT YOURSELF, GO HOSPICE!), she encouraged me to go back to LA so I could be on a Food Network television show called *Nailed It!* and a game show hosted by Meredith Vieira called *25 Words or Less*. But I told her that I was busy being with her. Making bank is NOT what Marilyn would do if she were in the same position. She would be there for her loved ones. So I'm sorry, Mom, that I didn't make a few thousand in cable residuals, but in this instance, you were (dead?) wrong.*

---

* You are right to question the quality and taste of this joke. But what if making a (dead) joke is the Funniest? What is the Funniest anyway? Is it the most unexpected, or is it, in fact, an unconsciously hoped-for, yes, extremely simple pun that ANYONE could think of? Just because it's low-hanging fruit—isn't that the reason it should be picked first? You could get one of those picking sticks with a grabber on the end to get the higher-hanging fruit and look more precocious, but I see the bruised apple on the ground and I grab it in my hands for guaranteed eating. I AM NOT CLEVER; my mother is dead. And she was wrong (in thinking that I should earn money instead of spending her last months alive with her). That means she was dead wrong. And that also makes you, in my assessment, MORTALLY MISTAKEN to question this comedic choice.

Like any leader, my mom had strong opinions—and I look for that now in friends, swing dance classes, the twelve-step cults. SHOW ME THE WAY! Someone who will tell me what the exact right thing is to do. For my mom, Nordstrom is GOOD. T.J.Maxx is GOOD. Ann Taylor is NOT GOOD. (Cheaply made? Store lighting? I don't know! Do not question it! HAVE FAITH!) Delta Airlines is GOOD. (Because it is based in Minnesota?) American Airlines is BAD. People whom my mother knows are GOOD. Anyone she doesn't know is SUSPECT until proven GOOD once she knows them ALMOST IMMEDIATELY. Once she gets more info on you, you gain value and she will describe you in glowing terms to spread the word. It wasn't until she died that I realized that what she called GOOD was arbitrary. GOOD means known, but it's also a conscious decision to see it as GOOD.

My mom will rehire the painter who drinks on the job and tramps Benjamin Moore on the wood floor because she decides that he is GOOD in some way: his wife had a kidney transplant, he's a mensch, or he understands color relationships. The point being, she doesn't know GOOD from BAD any more than I do—she just chooses to claim one thing as the best over another.

I take Delta and stay at Hilton properties (Hampton Inns, mostly) because they remind me of the GOOD that is my mother—even though I've had a few experiences that have been less than GOOD. (How does every Delta flight going back to LA stop in Atlanta even if you are starting in Salt Lake City? And I have stayed in a past-its-prime Hilton DoubleTree where I was refused a third cookie and there was an American melting pot–diverse variety of pubes surrounding the sweating toilet.) But my mom's certainty in the greatness of a person, place, or thing is what is great. I hope to be like her one day and choose to see the GREATNESS of everything in my path. But once I meet or have an experience or a product that my mom has said was GOOD, I argue that I kind of make it BAD with my presence.

This is my conundrum. My mom was The Best. The Greatest of All of the Times. She always picked up the phone! She planned our wedding and split the bill! She visited me in the psych ward every day and paged through *O* magazine for two hours sitting next to me—a trembly forty-year-old in pj's next to an orange plastic cigarette bucket! She went to my show any time I was within three hours' drive! She counseled me (*and* my friends)! She forgave me over and over again for being a killjoy on topics ranging from her love of God—

ME: Hey, Mom, What Would Jesus Buy? WWJB?

MOM: Aagh. Honey. Okay. Jesus probably wouldn't buy much, but if he did, he'd want it to be good quality.

ME: I bet Jesus loved a SALE!

MOM [*tired*]: Okay, honey. Hahaha.

—to mocking her anticipatory joy over anything—

MOM: Ever since I was a little girl [a common refrain], I've always wanted to go to the Russian Tea Room [Amsterdam in spring/buy a diamond solitaire from Tiffany/see a pope]!

ME: I thought ever since you were a little girl you wanted to stay at the Ritz-Carlton West Palm Beach.

MOM: I know. It's true. You laugh, but it's true.

My mom *is a baller. She went to therapy with me when I was a young adult (twenty-one)!*

The therapist asked her, ill-advisedly, "Marilyn, who's your favorite daughter?"

```
MOM: Well . . . Sarah.
```

Sarah's her favorite! I KNEW IT. And I get it. Her daughter Sarah didn't just ask her to drive six hours round trip to Minneapolis for an amateurish, confrontational bitch-slap. My mom then, LIKE A CHAMP—DESPITE BEING SET UP FOR A SUCKER PUNCH to the twat—stayed for the REST OF THE SESH to hear how her having a "favorite" daughter might be a problem.

My mom also:

- called me "cabbage sweetie" and my sister "pumpkin sweetie"!
- went to dance and violin lessons for six years with me! (She bowed out after that, claiming I was "old enough" to go on my own. Turns out I will never mature enough in self-motivated discipline and always need a crowd of witnesses to do anything.)
- made dinner, made sure we had plenty of everything, and kept a home's all-white interior clean and beautiful every year for sixty years!
- worked through issues with my dad and with us when times got tough!
- encouraged us to read and be interested in the arts and in people!

And on the other hand:

- My mom LOVED the phone—which means she loved talking to other people—sometimes more than her kids. I know she did plenty of other things, but her walking around the kitchen with her hand up to say "just a minute" while listening to a church/Bible-study/neighbor pal is my main recollection of her from childhood.
- She adored appearances—beauty, attractiveness, everything upscale. She had brand loyalty and wore a big diamond pendant necklace "so people can see me! You disappear after the age of fifty!"
- Because everything was white or fancy, Mom begged us to PICK UP YOUR STUFF! And our actual physical presence embodied part of that "stuff."
- My mom, seeing me lying in bed, would implore me to keep the SHEET BETWEEN MY SKIN AND THE QUILT because "YOUR SKIN HAS OILS!!!" I now have one of the quilts and am getting my oils all over it during my daily use.
- Our family was a reflection of her. If I had darker skin over my lip (called melasma), she was as uncomfortable as if SHE HERSELF had a shadowy pigment beneath her nose that could be read as lady mustache. Though I knew she loved us, she wasn't very physically affectionate unless it included a comment like (WHILE PETTING MY HEAD), "Comb your HAIR, honey." She would hug in a triangle form—shoulders first, as I continue to do today in her honor. She was diagnostic: "Honey, when you don't wear makeup, you look mentally ill!" At the same time, she was also known to solemnly pronounce about once a month,

> "You girls are the most beautiful, intelligent girls in the whole world." Sarah and Maria Bamford: revolting and repellent princess queens! My mom wasn't a huge kid fan, from what I can tell. She was a GREAT grandmother and mom, but I sometimes wondered if it had been a different era, whether she would have had kids at all. I cramped her style. My mom was really funny and sharp; she loved to travel and meet new people. She said she would have written a book herself if some asinine nincompoop hadn't burst her balloon animal when she showed a Duluth editor what she had written so far of a book. This dum-dum "editor" told her it wasn't any good. WHAT? EVERYTHING IS GOOD! May this unnamed critic be damned to hell or to writing a book of their own.

Mom's role as a charismatic leader also inspired a devotion to trying to please her. One of the best ways to do this was with news. Marilyn LOVED NEWS! And it had to be EXCEPTIONAL! Scott called this "Marilyn getting something in her beak"! And you couldn't predict what the showstopper would be.

If I called my mom and said I had just done a show in San Francisco, that might be good enough, but it might not quicken her breath or get her interrupting me for details. But if I did a show and a celebrity was in the audience—well, then. That goes in the beak! With this piece of tinfoil in her craw, she'd fly to her phone, telling everyone about it.

When I got this very book deal, I knew she wasn't feeling well because she just said, "Oh. [*Cough.*] Good for you, kiddo." A year before she died, I told her my work was featured in the *New York Times* and the *New Yorker* in the same week. Exhausted, she was not exactly blasé, but I had to repeat the news again to make sure she'd heard.

ME: Mom, I'm in the *New York Times* and the *New Yorker*. This week. IN ONE WEEK.

MOM: I know, honey, that's great. [*Struggling to breathe.*] I'm so . . . proud of you.

Yes, I nagged a mortally ill woman for additional recognition after her seventy-six years of service.

My mom is the reason I love showbiz. The very first time I got up in front of a crowd and everyone was looking at me, there was a WHOOSH of recognition! THIS IS NIIIIIIIZE. I'VE GOT SOMETHING IMPORTANT TO SHARE! MOMMA LOVES ME!

I chased the elation of maternal attention. I'm not good at cooking, being social, decorating, Christianity. But low-level celebrity? That I can deliver. Press in the *Duluth Budgeteer*? You got it. Niche podcast character? CAN DO. Once every five episodes on a hit series? NO PROBZ. How'd my sister Sarah get notice? She became a medical DOCTOR! A pathologist and mother of four. Ah . . . well played.

For my sister, being a medical professional made her beyond reproach for many years. But then, fifteen years in, my brave sister Sarah gave up physician-hood!!!!! And became a LIFE COACH/SHAMAN. In a small city like Duluth, that job change took a huge set of vag flaps. And boy was Mom bummed. Like, *pissed off.* I think Sarah managed to maintain favorite status by having a beautiful family, staying in Duluth, caring for my parents while they aged, and becoming a published author of SEVERAL books (which, as a shiny object, really sort of beats cutting up the dead into chunks). Please check out my sister's library of memoirs at www.followyourfeelgood.com, where she discusses the process of quitting medicine.

Back to making my mom human: not a big deal, as it was the '70s, but Mom did hit me across the face a few times. The first time it happened,

I was about eleven. It was after a violin lesson when we were in the car and I think I said something like, "Who CARES?" And the last time it happened I was twenty-one (also in the car), and I said, like, "Who the fuck CARES?" and she reached into the back seat and slapped me across the face, whereupon I got out of the car and walked ten blocks (to my parents' house, where they let me live for free) in protest.

My mom had some homophobia regarding loved ones (my dad, me), and I'm sure this was something that fed my intrusive thoughts. My fears that I might be attracted to the same sex were OFF THE CHAIN, sometimes trumping the fear of being a child-molesting mass murderer (which shows just how bad homophobia was at that time).

My mom always panicked that my dad might "read" gay to others. I don't think she was *really* concerned about his sexuality, but if he wore anything colorful or wildly patterned, it would be removed from his closet rotation (and driven to Goodwill on a midnight run). The most epic example of this happening was when my dad was getting ready for breakfast on his way to work in what was—at the time—his favorite shirt. It was a great shirt. It was a bright red, cotton seersucker, long-sleeved dress shirt with giant BLUE strawberries on it. I loved that shirt. It had been purchased in the late '60s but was still being worn in the early '80s. The conversation went like this:

MOM: Joel, do not wear that shirt.

DAD: I can wear whatever I want.

MOM: Joel, it's unprofessional.

DAD: Marilyn, you're trying to control me.

My dad went back to the fridge to get a drink of whatever lukewarm powdered-milk concoction he had chilling. As he closed the door, my mother came up from behind him with an open jar of mustard and proceeded to splash a heaping tablespoon of Dijon over his shoulder, resulting in a large dripping stain down his shirtfront. My dad, super pissed, went to my mom's china cabinet and took one plate after another and threw them on the floor. Maybe five in total broken. Not Lifetime TV material, but somewhat stressful.

Another time, my mom threw out a suitcase that was electric green (which Dad had bought on sale) because it looked "gay."

Aside from homophobia, heterosexual sex was also a touchy subject. My mom gave us the sex talk with a side of shame/fear of disease. My first joke was about how my mom prepped me before my first girl-boy party:

MOM: Sweetie, Bamfords get pregnant like falling off logs. Gonorrhea, syphilis, AIDS, genital warts, but oh, Jenny's mom is here to pick you up, well [*with a smile*], HAVE A GOOD TIME!

She was very strict about waiting to have sex till married, yet at the same time, Mom was very flirtatious/physical with my dad. She walked around nude and left the bathroom door open while sitting on the toilet. When my sister lost her virginity to her boyfriend in college, my mom (and therefore my sister) was DEVASTATED. Years later, Sarah and I read in my mom's journals (which my mom gave us permission to read) that she'd had sex with my dad on their first date. She wrote about it. Casually. And if she wrote about having sex with my dad on their first date (without any detectable anxiety), this means she had definitely had sex before meeting my dad. She was the only girl staying at the same trailer park for the summer, and he was only there for two weeks. So my parents' storied romance was just an extended one-night stand that ended up working out. I questioned her on this, and she had this to say:

MOM: Well, TECHNICALLY, I was a virgin.

I wanted more details, but she refused, and she's taken that technicality to the grave, leaving me with only my foul imagination to come up with salacious answers about my now-dead mother's adolescent sex life.

In the months before she died, my mom posted on Facebook a well-worn quote by Ralph Waldo Emerson on the definition of success:

> *To laugh often and much; to win the respect of the intelligent people and the affection of children; to earn the appreciation of honest critics and endure the betrayal of false friends; to appreciate beauty; to find the beauty in others; to leave the world a bit better whether by a healthy child, a garden patch, or a redeemed social condition; to know that one life has breathed easier because you lived here. This is to have succeeded.*

Whaaaaat? I love my mom. She was very kind and loving, but I'm not sure, at least to myself and my sister, that the topic sentence of her life's paragraph was "ENJOY!" What I learned from her was: PAY EVERYONE, SEND THANK-YOU NOTES, ALWAYS BRING A GIFT, and "KEEP IT HIGH AND TIGHT, AND SMILES, LADIES, SMILES!" Now she's telling me *we all have to* better the world with a "redeemed social condition"?? Jesus Christ Almighty, Marilyn Halverson Bamford.

RECIPE FOR MOM

This recipe is all about self-possession. You know what to do.

- FRESH mixed greens from the RIGHT PLACE
- GOOD goat cheese. YOU KNOW WHAT I MEAN!
- Sliced grapes, roasted walnuts. I'm not going to spell it out for you.

1. Make a tangy dressing of lemon juice, Dijon mustard, olive oil, and vinegar without measuring and toss with abandon.
2. Serve with GOOD bread, toasted with VERY GOOD olive oil/garlic. The most important thing about the bread is that no matter what you get or where it comes from, you MUST SAY it is THE BEST and WHY. The WHY can be anything: the story of how you found the store where you purchased the bread or about the type of bread, or some memory of being a little girl and always wanting to try that bread.
3. MAKE UP YOUR OWN GOOD and STAND FAST—YOUR EMOTION WILL CARRY THIS DISH!

4. Loose Cannon (and High Priest of Hilarity)

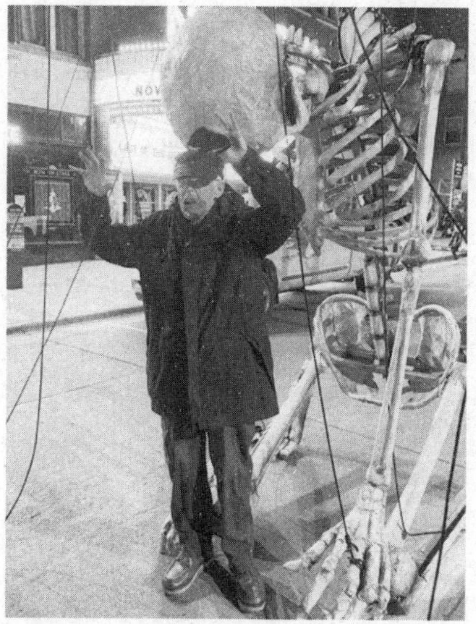

RECENT PHOTO OF MY DAD BEING HIMSELF (BENEATH A GIANT SKELETON PUPPET)

My mom called my dad a loose cannon. Every cult should have one. By "loose cannon," my mom meant that he is abrupt, obtuse, and confusing, i.e., a BLAST. He is also a series of sound effects: constantly shriek-sneezing and clearing his esophageal tract due to a less-than-funny chronic case of acid reflux.

When Scott and I were in Duluth while my mom was dying, I called my dad to say we were planning to stop by after dinner (my mom was already asleep).

DAD: [*Snort hack.*] I don't need you to come by. [*Grunt.*] I'm here alone, washing dishes. Whatever. [*Snort.*]

ME: So . . . does that mean we shouldn't come over?

DAD [*yelling*]: Dealer's choice! [*Blargh.*] I have soup and a can of tuna to share, but you're too tired and don't want to come see me.

ME: Dad, we're coming?

DAD: [*GRUNT.*] Okay, well, that's on you. I guess you don't need your privacy away from the old man. You're married now and need to attend to your relationship. [*HAAAAAACK!*] The Bible says cleave to thy husband.

ME: So you don't want us to stop by?

DAD: If you don't have time for your dad. [*SNORT!*]

ME: We're coming.

DAD: Okay. I'll try to stay awake. [*BLACCC-ERK!*]

People who have met both my father and me say that I am just like him. We share this explosive passive-aggressive dance, a sort of social bulimia, in which we simultaneously try to connect with someone (because we're lonely) and at the same time send the message that this person is UNDER NO OBLIGATION TO US WHATSOEVER. As I wave to you, I'm backing up. When I hand you a Christmas gift, I shout, "Feel free to regift or sell!" I sit down to talk with you at a party and either monologue my current act for forty-five minutes or s-l-o-w-l-y inch my way farther and farther away while lobbing a barrage of questions over an impenetrable wall of anxiety.

Another part of being a loose cannon is some egregious law-breaking. Yes, my dad shamefully fully utilizes the white man's pleasure of not only being able to afford any fines accrued while breaking a law but also the assumption that he will suffer no dangerous consequences. I am my father's daughter: I park illegally. A lot. It's not good. I once parked illegally at Los Angeles International Airport for ten whole days—in front of a fire hydrant, no less—because I didn't want to miss a flight to Phoenix. I got a sixty-five-dollar ticket. That I had the luxury of being able to pay. I rationalize this irresponsibility by telling myself that my tickets are generating revenue for the city (even though I may have put possibly thousands of lives in danger due to the blocking of an emergency water supply)? That is, of course, narcissism. "I CAN'T POSSIBLY FOLLOW LAWS THAT MAKE SOCIETY FUNCTION, 128 PEOPLE NEED TO SEE ME IN SCOTTSDALE ON A THURSDAY NIGHT!"

In the same vein, at the height of the pandemic and against all travel advisories, my parents came to visit us in California for eight weeks. When I took them to an In-N-Out Burger, my dad removed the plastic DO NOT SIT tape blocking the restaurant tables, scooted himself into a booth, and made himself comfortable. My mom and I protested and sat in the car. We left it to a twelve-dollar-an-hour staff member to explain to my father—a grumpy old white hearing-impaired retired RESEARCH DOCTOR—that he had to move due to a worldwide pandemic. And then, when he was crunchy about it, no one called the cops and he wasn't killed.

My dad's eccentricity (asshattery?) could be hard on my mom. When I was eleven, my parents took us on a road trip to Wyoming. On the way out, my sister played the same Styx *Greatest Hits* tape over and over again out of the speakers of a cassette player that was the size of a hardback book. We all could sing along to the piercing male soprano of "Babe" and church-organ virtuosity of "Fooling Yourself (The Angry Young Man)." Halfway there, Sarah found out that the Grand Tetons means "Big Boobs" in French, and as we crossed the border from South Dakota to Wyoming she started yelling, "Big Tits! Big Tits!" My father joined in. In a competing performance, my mom would read aloud from the conservative preacher Dr. (PsyD, not MD) James Dobson's book *Focus on the Family for Teens.* Here's a quick selection for your enjoyment. (Read it aloud on a road trip with a disgruntled teenager!!)

> *Deaden the evil desires lurking within you. Have nothing to do with sexual sin, impurity, lust, and shameful desires. God's terrible anger is upon those who do such things.*

My sister and I were eleven and fourteen at the time, for perspective. This mélange was our family's alternative to the VW bug arm-punching game.

On the way to hiking, we stopped to see Old Faithful. On this trip, as was traditional, my mom was charged with the heavy lifting: she organized, motivated, disciplined, comforted, while we all whined and generally disrespected her efforts. I hope heaven is a five-star all-inclusive resort where my mom is allowed hours of uncriticized shopping and reading Scripture aloud.

Like every good customer-service professional I've ever talked to, my mom had the measured delivery of someone who is finding their self-esteem elsewhere due to the onslaught of negative feedback. My mom's common response was a mellifluous, flouncy, "Sorry, sorry, sorry!!!!" And it's not that she didn't mean it, there are just only so many times you can take full responsibility for someone's displeasure. I try to emulate that trait unless I am being schooled on a human-rights issue.

About fifteen years before she died, my mom gifted me four beautifully boxed fancy Paper Source celadon-green files containing the curated onion-paper archives of my entire life in letters, photos, articles, finger-painting explorations. (This is on top of doing a HUGE "Life" scrapbook of my existence until the age of forty that took her a year to complete.)

But don't kid yourself: this gift was a burden in disguise!

"You're going to need this when you write a book," said my mother.

"YOU WRITE A BOOK, GODDAMMIT!" I yelled.

"Sorry, sorry, sorry! Sigh."

Upon moving, I unceremoniously dumped her carefully tabbed historic time line into a large plastic tub from Office Depot and put it in our basement. Later, when I told her about the book deal while she had lung cancer, I had the NERVE to ask my mom if she could remember where some photo of my junior prom might be. And then, she, WHILE DYING, tried to remember.

Therefore, on this road trip in the early '80s, a thousand miles in the car, my mom must have been pushed to the breaking point, because she announced, "I need to take a break from you guys! Ever since I was a little girl, I've always wanted to have a fancy lunch, alone, at the Old Faithful Inn in Yellowstone National Park." She departed, and we were left alone with Dad.

My dad has always prompted us to call him "the Best Dad in the Whole World." He calls my sister "the Best Oldest Daughter in the Whole World." I'm "the Best Youngest Daughter in the Whole World." It's reciprocal propaganda, but it's true, he is a good guy. He's always been active in our community: trying to help out with mentoring local kids, teaching English to immigrants arriving in Duluth, working with men just out of prison for domestic violence crimes. He sends me cards and cookies, he taught me to drive, he taught me how to change a tire nine times (it didn't take) and chop wood. He attended every play, every concert. All that is true. It is also true that on this trip in the sixty minutes we were away from my mother, he broke a federal law and may have committed a misdemeanor for child endangerment.

We had an hour to kill and started walking around Geyser Park's wooden walkways with my dad, eating gingersnaps from a torn-open bag. The geysers were roped off and there were huge signs everywhere that read DANGER AREA and KEEP OUT: FRAGILE THERMAL RESERVE. The geysers varied in size, anywhere from a teacup to a Subaru in diameter, and they had creative names like Scheherazade's Spout and The Singing Donut. They spewed randomly. In 2016, a twenty-three-year-old died by falling into one called Porkchop. Eventually, we came upon a salad bowl–depth geyser unfortunately named The Irishman's Geyser.

"I wonder if the Irishman is hungry," my dad said. Then he tossed a gingersnap into one of the seven natural wonders of the Western Hemisphere. We thought this was hilarious. He tossed in a few more and we watched each one disintegrate in God's creation. Then my dad got an idea.

"Hey, Sarah, go see how hot it is."

My sister—at my dad's request—went under the ropes, jumped off the wooden boardwalk, and dipped her sweatshirt in the hissing Irish pot.

"It's hot!"

We were not stopped by security. After feeding the Irishman, my dad decided it would be fun if *he* had some alone time. My dad—and this was common—faded away in the crowd and hid from us. My dad loves to do this: to vanish for ten to fifteen minutes and then suddenly reappear. It's a slow-moving peekaboo or immersion exercise in abandonment. In a bad father, this could be the sign of having a secret second family, but my dad always came back from these short lessons in object impermanence with some sort of hard candy. We were okay, but now—as a person who knows people who have kids—I think, "Huh." I like to dissolve into the distance—a few lengths from loved ones—myself. Scott and I will be at the airport and I will weed off, melting into the seething humanity that is LAX. I won't say anything, I just leave and keep my eye on him. I test my freedom. I see how far and wide I can roam while still retaining the company of my husband in a chaotic international hub. He finds this unnerving. "Where are you?" he'll text me. *I'm 6 feet behind you, watching you from behind this potted palm.* And now he doesn't worry as much, because he knows that when I return from my brief ghosting, I'll have purchased myself a stuffed big-eyed comfort animal and a bag of Cheez-Its to share.

As a kid, I was very close with my dad. I think we were best friends? We'd go on long hikes, and he'd listen to my atrocious violin playing and any speech I'd prepare to run for school offices, which was every office, every year. In retrospect, my dad was almost as depressed as I was. Here's the tone of the poetry he was sharing with me at the time:

I

I find myself, here, again
two weeks after stopping Prozac

They are back: an edgy anger
which makes me wrankle, at the neck
an rheumanant brain
which brings me to the same subject, again and again
a too quick brain, hard not to like, but
which presents an edged, inappropriate humor
a self distrust, of the above
which blocks a sense of natural flow, freedom to express
what I had come to believe is me

I do not like those parts of me:
a racing, misguided, panic feeling
which my heart, it's pulse, does not relate or respect
taking up my time for fondness, sensing and savoring
shaking me awake roughly to search for meditative anodynes
opiates of prayer and writing down
which fill unread books of self observation and affirmation
that *little me* voice, 'I'm uncared for'
I am inattended, unobserved, passed over
I am insignificant, non-reactive and, in measure - massless
the voice which brings forth a petulant, plaint rasping at others
notice now, stop what you are doing, see me
'I am needy and you are necessary for that fulfilling of me'

I was right there with him! Life sucks! I suck! My pops was functional and able to keep a full-time doctor job and take care of us and have a connected, loving relationship with my mom—so maybe not deeply depressed, but downtrodden enough to come up with the phrase "ruminant brain." FYI, my dad's all-time favorite quote is by Golda Meir, former prime minister of Israel: "Don't be so humble—you're not that great."

I never met my grandparents. I don't know where my dad's personality came from, so all I have is his fan-fiction version of his childhood in Manhattan. Grandma Bamford was a psychiatric nurse as well as an alcoholic (my dad remembered that when he was a kid, there was always a full case of whiskey beneath the kitchen sink that was refilled monthly), and his dad was a psychiatrist who, near the end of my dad's time in high school, began experiencing what my dad thinks was early-onset Alzheimer's. My gramps Bamf tried to hide his quickly deteriorating professional abilities (my dad watched his doctor father on rounds try to revisit the same patients he had just seen minutes ago). From what my dad observed, my grandparents isolated themselves from their friends so no one would know Grandpa's brain was slowly being eaten by plaque. Grandpa—at around fifty—shouldn't have been working anymore. In his early sixties, my grandpa died of a stroke in a care facility. Then my grandma died by fire as a result of drinking, smoking, and then passing out in bed.

STOP **Now, that's not uncommon. We all watched *Mad Men*: alcoholism and secrets defined the 1950s! But here comes the yuck part: my dad's older sister, Joel Lee (who has since passed away), added a very destabilizing context to this family history when she got to the age that I'm at now, fifty-two. My aunt Joel Lee—like everyone in my family—loved a cult. She changed her full name four times, her final choice being Julie Anne Matheson. (She never went with anything showy, like "300" or "Peasebottom.") She did EST, Overeaters Anonymous, the Diamond Approach, Lazaris. Lazaris is a two-thousand-year-old spirit channeled through a Florida man named Jach Pursel, who was later accused of killing his ex-wife and her new husband but never did jail time. When my aunt got into Lazaris,**

Jach, or I guess "Lazaris," told her TONS OF STUFF ABOUT HER LIFE SHE DIDN'T KNOW ABOUT! And it was super-specific and gross! Lazaris said that the reason my aunt Joel Lee felt so bad her whole life was because she was molested by my grandfather as an infant, though she had never had any inkling of it before. And just to make sure she knew the DL, Lazaris, a Jesus-aged spirit inside and a generic white dude outside, told my aunt in explicit, nasty detail each moment of what happened as her grandfather and his friend "The Banker" violated her infant body while standing over her crib, which is, as this font reads, Sans Comic.

Now, from my dad's POV, his childhood was the bomb. At the age of five, my dad started a "cookie club." That is ingenious. He told his mom he wanted her to make cookies and have kids over and then start a club where once a week, he and his friends would meet at each other's homes and eat cookies. Then it happened. All the moms made cookies and had kids over every week. I wonder now if my whole life has just been striving for the lifestyle that is "COOKIE CLUB."

Suffice to say, Aunt Joel Lee was a divisive personality. She tried to get my dad to divorce my mom at one point in the '70s by refusing to leave their home for weeks. During an Ayn Rand–ian kick, she left us alone when she was supposed to babysit because she thought a four- and one-year-old could take care of themselves for an afternoon. When I moved to California, she called me. She wanted to make clear that she had "chosen" family and felt no obligation to biological family. She then invited me for dinner, and post–no-sugar, no-flour vegan meal where she told me I was a 7 in numerology, she loaded my car up with a garbage bag full of super-size Tampax that she no longer needed.

There are similarities between Joel Lee and me: she liked to do voices (she'd "channel" her own spirits sometimes!), she was in no way maternal (I wish I was cuddly but I am not), and we have the same scoliosis-hunched back that my dad shares. I try to make sure that I'm not like her (by sending gifts to all my nieces and nephews and contacting my sister and dad regularly). It has long been my fear that now I AM THE DIFFICULT OUTSIDER in the family. The takeaway I get from this ongoing cycle is: there's always going to be a black sheep and it may as well be you. Do whatever you want. If your initial crowd has a penchant for blackballing, do not be surprised if you look down and you have a number 8 on your shiny black belly.

STOP **Whenever I hung out with my aunt Joel Lee—and it wasn't often—she would, within five minutes of us beginning to chat, bring up her recovered memories in the same precise and troubling detail that had been given to her by Lazaris. It's a bracing opener. When I introduced Scott to her and her husband, James, over dinner, I forgot to give Scott a warning about this habit of hers, and after four minutes of small talk about vegan meatloaf, my aunt dove into the play-by-play story of her being raped as a baby. Though my dad loved his sister (my aunt) and respected that she needed to express her suffering, he didn't totally believe that the memory was real. I want to believe her. And she was a pill to our family for most of her life, so that would be a great justification for being that pill. #BELIEVEALLWOMEN. Whether or not anything happened, the takeaway is my aunt thought their childhood was abusive and was pissed about it, and my dad disagreed and was a loving pop. Everybody's dead now, Jach Pursel's Lazaris cult has largely been scrubbed from the internet, and we will never know.**

I never tried to argue with her history or her Diamond Approach society, Lazaris, Enneagrams, the time when she claimed she could fly while doing yoga or EST. Codependency is a huge part of continued inclusion in church potlucks. I'm lucky that the other main players didn't get book deals. I get to write stuff down—so you get my perspective in print. And really, isn't the Bible a self-published memoir of sorts? This is the Maria Bamford version of the Holy Scripture—like the King James version, but with less through line.

Before my mom died, she gave us a verbal list of women she thought Dad should date. And now, after six sessions with a grief counselor and support group, Dad has asked out every single age-appropriate lady within walking distance—only some of whom were on the list. (A bunch of them turned him down! I get it. You're seventy-seven, you've already had a husband for forty-five years, you don't want anyone cutting in on your mahjongg time.)

He now, after two years of my mom being gone, has a lovely partner named Mary. Mary brings me dirty, used white elephant gifts (a water-damaged children's book about pugs, a wooden frog mask with a broken head strap) every time I see her and then tells me I can throw them away immediately! She is good people.

My dad's responses in grief have been surprising. He's been extremely enterprising and creative in dealing with the loss of his partner of sixty years. When he's lonely, he bakes bread and brings it around the neighborhood. He rented a giant camper and traveled to Arizona by himself before realizing it was the middle of the quarantine and nothing was open. Without my mom, there is an untethering—he's painted a wall blue, moved the furniture, and dived into his friendships ("Why don't men ever want to talk about what's really going on?" *I don't know, Poppi.*) I don't think he's happier, but he has times of happiness, and that does help to teach me about how to stick around in life after the worst thing happens. He is now attending an outpatient treatment program for depression and anxiety and getting on meds again at eighty-two. Keep going, kid.

RECIPE FOR DAD

This all must be done in secret or with an air of secrecy, but witnessed by one other person.

1. Grab a huge generic duplex sandwich cookie pack while grocery shopping. Open as soon as you take it from the shelf. Eat one row of the cookies. Hand the opened package to the clerk to scan. The cashier sometimes comments on it and it's fun.
2. Stop at the drugstore. Assign a task to your companion. For example: Retrieve Icy Hot cream. Hide somewhere in the store for around five to eleven minutes. Come back with an open half-empty bag of pink puffy circus peanuts that are stale.
3. Make cookies without a recipe and mail them out in white plastic shopping bags in a "poucher." Call everything a poucher.
4. For years, make hundreds of pouchers of these tough oatmeal-raisin nuggets bound by veins of unmixed flour and share them with neighbors, mail them across the country, hide them in your own home from your daughter Maria. She will find them.

OR

COOKIE CLUB

1. Set a day every week, like MONDAY NIGHT.
2. Tell everyone you know that you have a Monday-night cookie club.
3. LMK what happens.

5. My Sister: The Funny (Chosen) One

Jeff Fifield

Just this year I received a message on Facebook from a classmate I had not heard from in thirty-five years. It was from a fellow Suzuki violin survivor, Ramona Nazrani. Ramona is a fine human being and I'm sure she in no way meant to pry open a scab, poke at the gash beneath, and salt it:

> Hey, Maria, we were having an FB discussion on whether you were funny as a kid or not. Any comments? I said you were smart, but I thought Sarah was funnier and more perfect.

No "Hello! How are you?" Here are some ways I could respond:

1. A gif of a screaming monkey baby.
2. Ramona, who exactly is this "we" you mention? You and seven other people from the hockey cheerleading squad? Why are they not cc'd?
3. Ramona. We were in Suzuki together for *ten years*. That qualifies as classical-music combat duty. We (metaphorically?) slogged across the beaches of all three Seitz concertos and now you're going to query whether or not *I should have made it as a comedian*? We played "Allegro"—a mind-numbing original by Shinichi Suzuki—on repeat in any old folks' home that would let us in the door and NOW you're COMING AT ME?

The honest answer to Ramona's question is: Yes. YES, YES, RAMONA! My sister was/is way funnier than I am. She is also more confident, energetic, regularly creative, and functional than I'll ever be. She's thinner, she's better dressed, more organized. The editors had some real problems with this chapter about my sister because they thought my descriptions of our relationship are too banal, too typical of sisters, not dramatic enough. That is exactly what is so bizarre about it! It is that these tiny-tiny-tiny things that go on between us feel like tsunamis of "compare and despair." Examples:

1. My sister always makes food for everybody. She makes a bunch of homemade food and puts it out like it's no big deal. IT IS A FUCKING BIG DEAL. Recently, she invited us on a picnic, didn't ask me to bring anything (I didn't), and yet she brought 2 (TWO) different kinds of delectable handmade

sandwiches, organic cherries, salad, a cold VARIETY of drinks, AND cookies. She hauled it all to an idyllic river setting she found outside Duluth and laid it out on a blanket. At no time did she stop and say, "HEY! YOU GUYS! CHECK OUT ALL OF THIS STUFF I JUST DID FOR YOU ASSHOLES!"

(I have ONLY ONCE made my family dinner, though I am constantly swaggering about my self-serving good deeds. If I have done anything, you will know about it and I will have photographic proof. In my defense, I have picked up the check for family dinners and then tried to write it off as a business expense.)

2. My sister is always the last person to get served. I eat the dropped egg bits off salad-bar buffets while cutting the line. I raise my fork to eat my husband Scott's food before his plate has hit the table. I have eaten food LEFT BEHIND on strangers' tables. And I have eaten someone's leftover room service—you know, the stuff that's left outside their door, when you have to lift up the silver domes, or unfold the napkinned baskets of rolls that sit at either side of the dark hallways of hotels, to reveal what delights lie within like treasure chests in a magical cave?
3. My sister keeps five-dollar bills to give to people on the street.
4. Sarah came to visit me in the psych ward. This is even though I have been doing a comedic impersonation of her onstage that she didn't like . . . for a full decade. That's five years past the point when she asked me not to do an impersonation of her. She continues to talk to me despite the fact that I publicly make fun of things that mean a lot to her, like spirituality, life coaching, ayahuasca ceremonies, shamanism. And

now, and I'm not sure of this, but I'm pretty sure she'll still talk to me after I write about her in a book. I am, in fact, banking on this assumption.

5. She listened to my two-hour audiobook. *I* haven't listened to my audiobook! After listening, she complimented it kindly over the phone in a detailed voice-mail message I have SAVED! I have only skimmed her books before feeling overwhelmed. As with all books, I pass swiftly over the text, pausing only for prurient details. From what I've been able to take in, her books are really beautiful, AND there's a great scene in one memoir where she is naked on the floor trying to have some private time to shove a hemorrhoid application up her bum and her four kids break the door down. But a lot of her writing features an experience of spirituality that I do not have, and so I tab through, alighting only upon anything foul. She *shouldn't* be kind to me or take any interest in my life's work, as I am not generous enough to mindfully take a minute for hers. She's seen a thousand of my shows. She NEVER HAS TO SEE A SHOW EVER! She's my *sister*, which means she has been forced to listen to my schtick on a regular basis for over fifty years.

I am terrified to write about my sister. She has asked me not to talk about her in my comedy act. I sort of stopped? But a book is different! And she's written about me. So it's okay? I guess I will find out. BTW, my sister is not an alarming person. If you've met her, you know that she is positive, helpful, funny. At the same time, she *is* my older sister. I always have this feeling that she—in some way that I'll never be able to guess at and reform—is nauseated and repulsed by me. She most likely isn't. Or if she is, she's nice enough to keep it to herself.

Hey, Maria, do you harbor some type of irrational resentment toward your wonderful sister regarding something small that occurred in childhood? Of course. But I brought it up twenty years ago to her via a handwritten letter by mail! She then apologized profusely—in writing—on a note card with a sad terrier puppy cover.

I already covered this, but for background's sake:

When my sister was going to seventh grade in 1970s Duluth, there was a practice of boys giving young ladies "titty twisters" as well as "sharking" them (pulling down their pants to reveal their genitalia). She was not having the best time. She got involved with booze, pot, and learning to sew her own velour sweatshirts. As a result of the stress at school, Sarah brought home some of these teasing behaviors in the form of sudden breast-grabbing and taunting that there was something "wrong" with me, mentally or gender-wise. She called me Fred and suggested I might be a boy (I had short hair, a flat chest) or that I was certifiably insane. Typical big-sister/little-sister crap.

In the realm of damaging human experiences, it's ludicrous. This is a tiny trauma with a small "t." And certainly nothing that should be memorable, much less memoir-able. If I'd had any sort of reality check of what was happening in households all around me (severe physical abuse, sex addiction, the industrial breeding of Labrador retrievers), maybe that would have contextualized my experiences. Or, with my head chemistry, it might have just proved to me that the world was an Eville and Dangerouse place wherein I was a part of the problem. In any event, I felt real bad. In the eyes of my cool sister, it seemed, something was monumentally wrong with me. Through no fault of my sister's typical older-sibling treatment of me, my intrusive thoughts from OCD blossomed off this stuff. Of course I now feared that I was going to reach out and touch a female person—relative, friend, or stranger—because that had happened and was happening to me.

This is the part of the memoir where you go, "That's it? You just got a couple of nip twongs?" Yup. That is it. And being the grocery-store orchid that I am, it broke me. My husband and I always joke that if I was in a survival situation on a raft floating in the Pacific, I'd be the first person to jump off, swim to a shark, and pry open its mouth. I am not a fan of long-haul discomfort.

AN ILLUSTRATION OF MY FEELINGS FROM THIS TIME

And despite the fact that my sister treated me poorly, I'd sit whining like a dog outside her bedroom door to try to hang out with her. Yes, I asked for it! "It" being any sort of attention. "And where were your mother and father?" It was the '70s! *Lord of the Flies* parenting! The kids will work it out on their own!

The pinnacle of this time occurred during my sister's eighth-grade year at a public junior high (my parents would later transfer her to a tiny Catholic private school to get her off the pipe). One day, my sister and her friends were building on the story line that I was "crazy." To someone on an even keel, that's water off a duck's back. The proper reply in that debate would be, "No I'm not. YOU'RE crazy. And here's why!" But, delicate grocery-outlet arrangement that I was, I was devastated. Was I crazy? Am I crazy?

My sister and a pal, when I wouldn't leave them alone to hang out in my sister's room, took theatrical action. They tied me to my bed (with loose gym socks—I could have easily gotten out). They told me I couldn't escape or else the "men in the white coats" would come. They closed the door, presumably to walk to the local drugstore and shoplift Bonne Bell Lip Smacker products. I lay there. I could have left. But I stayed, tied up, saturated in self-loathing, certain that I was a certified lunatic. After about twenty to thirty minutes of perseverating and pretending that I hadn't already freed myself, I got out of my bed and made myself a Big Gulp–size ice cream sundae with microwaved peanut butter to eat in front of *Happy Days* on TV. Soon after this episode, my sister switched schools, lost interest in teasing me, and gained an interest in scholastics, cheerleading, and being a more pleasant person.

Our relationship isn't distinctive at all! It only demonstrates that despite having a French vanilla Häagen-Dazs life experience, I've spun whatever I've gotten into vindictive martyrdom.

🛑 SIDEBAR. As a nonparent, may I very judgmentally hazard a suggestion for harm reduction and violence prevention? Parenting is a massive job. That said, I think it's best that children aren't left to "work it out on their own." Check in on them in the basement every forty-five minutes or so. "Every forty-five minutes? But I'm a skin-care specialist!" I know. You're grinding cheddar to keep them in leather kicks. But they are also BABY ANIMALS WITH TEETH.

I KNOW it isn't convenient to care for a two-legged hot dog twenty-four hours a day. I DON'T WANT TO DO ANYTHING EITHER. EVER. Put down your international pager every hour or so to see where your toddler lefty or sixteen-year-old righty has waddled off to. And if you choose to have a more laissez-faire attitude, don't be surprised when ten years later your kid reveals to you that some seriously jacked-up roughhousing happened while you were less than a hundred feet away on the phone telling a friend how much you love your kids. Have a little curiosity about the screaming or the five hours a day on the internet your daughter Addison is DMing an Instabot, wiring her babysitting money for the promise of a foot-modeling career. And yes, her flip-flopped feet are now on the dark web.

Back to Sarah. If it sounds like I'm trying to make my sister seem perfect, yes and yes. She IS perfect because she is not ME. She is GOOD, I am BAD. And more specifically, my sister and I—though we love each other—don't agree on quite a few things. My sister is a professional spiritual person, a retired doctor, and now a painter. I am an atheist and a comedian. But we are both respectful of each other's beliefs to the best of our awkward abilities.

There is a reason Sarah asked me to stop doing jokes about her. Sarah lives in Duluth—which is like living inside of a kaleidoscope—where every day you see old reflections of what people have learned about you through the course of your entire life. "Sarah, did you hear the joke Maria made about you in 1998?" Yes, she did! And she'd rather not hear about it when she's getting her teeth cleaned, or at a neighbor's Christmas party after you've had three mulled wines and are trying to touch the small of her back. I told her she can write about me freely in her books. And I can afford to be that generous emotionally because I *never* hear about what people think of me in the sprawling strip mall that is Los Angeles. You want to speak ill of me about something I said sixty seconds ago? Grab the mic and run the light. You live in MONTROSE, Wendy! I will NEVER see you IRL.

Like everyone in the Bamford familia, Sarah has an extremely strong worldview she is trying to sell you on. She would like you to connect with animal totems. My dad would like you to get "brain coaching" from his formerly felonious pal and author, Wilbur Fryberger. I would like you to join a twelve-step program, admit there is no God, try stand-up, or thank me for being alive. My mom would have liked you to shop only at Nordstrom (NEVER THE RACK—IT'S A SCAM) and to travel with Hilton, Delta, and Hertz. We're a band of persuasives.

So you can imagine that when my mom was dying, everybody had their "road less traveled" they wanted Marilyn to be on. In her final months, my dad kept trying to get my mom to do relationship workbook exercises. I tried to get my DYING MOTHER to listen to my audiobook. "I'm sure [*cancer cough-cough*] it's wonderful, honey. . . ." And my sister tried to get my lifelong Jesus freak mother to get her chakras in order. So at the end of my mom's life, we were all, in our own aggressive manipulations, bossing her around.

My sister also gave my mom a talking-to:

SARAH: Hey, Mom, it's okay to let go. . . . You can leave us. We're going to be okay.

I don't remember what Marilyn said in response, but my mom—even up to the last minute—was not into "letting go." She LOVED living. Thankfully, Mom would NOT be intimidated by either me ("DON'T DIE!") or my sister ("OKAY TO DIE!") and ended up dying, in her own sweet time, about a week later, when she felt like it.

As with most sibling relationships, nothing really "happened" or "is happening" that is out of the ordinary between myself and my sister; it just FEELS catastrophic. In my mind, I am a harpooned whale; I am the overweight, arthritic pit bull struggling out of her dog bed for string cheese; I am the glassed-in viper at the zoo—alone, biting at dead flesh in the dark. And Sarah is a lighted vitrine—all beauty and possibility. The feelings do not match the facts at all.

Back in Duluth, my mom now dead, we were having snacks and drinks on my dad's porch. The topic of conversation was unimportant, because I was not the topic. The main speakers were my sister and my dad. Apparently, I hadn't gotten enough attention recently, because I found myself getting up WHILE THEY WERE TALKING and doing five push-ups in the center of where everyone (Scott, brother-in-law Mark, Sarah, four nieces and nephews) was sitting. There was some confusion as to what was happening. I explained, "Oh, I think I just wanted attention. I can do push-ups!"

My push-ups were then complimented by my dad and hub: "Good job, wow, etc.," in the way that you encourage a toddler learning to walk. Upon which my sister, Sarah, said, "You know, I do ten push-ups every day when I wake up as a part of my normal routine." So she's in the game. Then she and my dad went right back into talking about a previous topic that was not me. I then GOT DOWN ON THE DECK AGAIN and did five more push-ups.

The competition between us, of course, began with my mom's desire for gleaming *objets du triomphe.* My beaked mom would light up and take hold of any freshly foraged worm of accomplishment either of us brought home. For me, I played the violin: that was the wriggling prey I brought back to the nest. But Sarah was charming, extroverted, and not mental, and had good grades. She had more of a worm *farm*. My mom had high hopes for me, but they were tempered by my abilities: maybe I could MARRY a doctor or just be seen as a good person (very different from actually being a good person). Perhaps I'd be capable of dressing attractively or cleaning a bathroom. I accomplished only one thing on that list in that I know how to hire someone to help me clean the bathroom. My sister has done *all* the things. (Her husband is also a doctor! She shoots, she scores!)

Bamfords express their love through a constant assignment of chores. As soon as I get home, my dad hands me a shovel or a rag or sends me to the garage for pliers and then it's time to do something well until completion. Consecutive urgent projects follow until bedtime. And because my parents are by turns anxious (Mom) and depressed (Dad), the list is never completed. There will also be a running commentary on how these assignments might be done better than in the way you are currently doing them.

At one point in her lung-cancer fight, my mom assigned her daughters the immediate addition of an Emergency Birdhouse to the Front Lawn so she could Fully Experience a Beautiful Bird-Filled View from Her Hospice Bed. My mom already had three birdhouses in the backyard, but none could be seen from her bed. And we couldn't just move one from the backyard, which is what my pathetic (and lazy) pitch had been. It had to be perfect! And my mom was right! If I'm shuffling off the mortal coil, I'd like to have a front-row seat to some wild animals exploring brand-new playground equipment. My mom's dying wish was to have a birdhouse that matched her and my dad's fawn-gray house, one that would attract the right birds, the best—which I think is "cardinals." And as with all jobs done in my family, there is a somehow perfect way of doing it (in my mind) that one (me) can't figure out.

But do not worry! Sarah the competent one is on the case! She drives IMMEDIATELY to a store in Duluth—a specialty BIRD SHOP! (Who knew? Sarah did!) It somehow has the Best Birdhouse in the World: four tiers, suet, seed, open-plan multispecies hangout areas. She has the whole thing up in forty-five minutes. I help out a little bit by getting some wires from the garage to jury-rig a missing bird perch. I also broke up the cardboard boxes and threw them in the recycling bin. And all the while I was doing those things, I felt troubled that I was going to do something "BAD" that would somehow dishonor, harm, ruin, and generally F up the whole deal. And of course, I did. My sister asked me to open the birdseed bag, then drag over a tarp to make sure that none of the seed got on the lawn when I poured it into the feeder. I did not pull the tarp over. I thought, as I often do, "I CAN DO IT! I CAN POUR ALL THE SEED IN WITHOUT SPILLING." Predictably, a half cup of birdseed spilled out onto the pristine grass.

```
SARAH: You need to clean that up, because it
    will grow into weeds.
ME [internal organs]: AAAAAAAAAAAAAAAAAAAAAAAAAA-
    AAAAAAAAAH!
```

I picked up SOME of the seeds, yes. But not ALL of the seeds. Why? Because I had this real belief (as I do with all authoritarian commands) that "it didn't matter." Even if weeds do grow, doesn't the lawn get mowed every two weeks? If mowed, won't the weeds be short, so short that they will for all intents and purposes, and even to the most important eyes of our loving mother dying six feet away behind a window, LOOK LIKE GRASS? The desperate attempt for perfection combined with an underlying resentful rebellion toward anything perfect is really my familial role in a nutshell lying errant on an otherwise spotless lawn.

(I'm the animal in the following photo.)

RECIPE FOR MY SISTER

Tater Tot hot dish! It is so easy to make!

You will fail.

You will also want Sarah to eat first, but she won't. She's not like that. She can wait, like a lady.

1. Get a pound of hamburger. Worry about what a pound is, read the label, but still feel uncertain. Is it a pound? Is it a hamburger? Feel insecure throughout. Pick up a package of meat and put it back three times. Feel bad that you are even buying hamburger, after all of the documentaries on food production and animal welfare you've seen. Think of scrapping the recipe altogether and ordering eight veggie subs from Subway like you always do. But know that will be another way to fail. Everybody's "okay" with Subway. But no one is ever really glad you brought it (unless they are on a twelve-hour nonunion commercial shoot or under the age of eighteen).
2. In the same store, get one can of mushroom soup. Shut off your rational mind. Know in your bones that you've gotten the "wrong kind" of mushroom soup. Read the recipe again. Mushroom soup, can of. Look at all the types of soup. Pick what looks like, from the label, the "best." Once you've picked this "best" can, it is now the "worst," because you have picked it. Put it back. Pick up another brand. Your picking of any brand has the same effect. You cannot pick the right can of mushroom soup. Buy six different brands.
3. Pick a bag of frozen Tater Tots. REPEAT ABOVE CONSUMER BOX STEP. There are fewer companies that manufacture Tater Tots and so less time spent! Buy three bags of Tater Tots, not knowing which one will "win" and be used.

4. Repeat for shredded cheese. Feel in your heart/head/lingam that extra-sharp cheddar is not the right choice. GO AGAINST THE RECIPE, WHICH JUST CALLS FOR "CHEESE," and get extra-sharp cheddar. Stop your cart. Google pizza places in your zip code in an effort to have a plan B. You said you were going to make dinner and goddammit, you're going to do it. You're going to feed eight people for the first time in your life with your own two hands. Back in the car home from the grocery store, get angry to the point of crying.
5. Brown the ground beef (cook till when you eat some it seems like how it should seem).
6. Add THE BEST-NOW-WORST mushroom soup and mix it around real nice.
7. Pour meat slosh into a casserole dish.
8. Pour THE BEST-NOW-WORST frozen Tater Tots over to cover it.
9. Cover Tater Tots with a layer of THE WRONG cheese.
10. Put in the oven at 375°F for one hour.
11. Serve to your family with tap water. Tell them three times that you made it from scratch. Feel bad that you didn't make a vegetable, a salad, or a dessert. They're cool about it, but it's a lot of salt and you've got to keep that tap water coming. Sarah doesn't need dessert anyway, because she's not really "into" food anymore. It's just fuel. She likes being present in her body and mind.
12. When your family leaves, eat all the burnt cheese along the edges of the casserole dish and wash down your meds with a Diet Coke.
13. Never again.

6. The Temple of Thin!

As mentioned, if you meet a member of my family, they will try to sell you on a point of view. My mom was Christianity/Tripadvisor, my dad "CORE VALUES." I'm for improv classes, and my sister would like you to try natural hallucinogens in Peru.

However, the underpinning spiritual dogma that has burned its way into my corpus callosum is, FOR CHRIST'S SAKE, BE THIN.

My own lifelong adventure with weight loss started when I got back from violin camp at nine years of age and happened upon the *Richard Simmons' Never-Say-Diet Book* on a living-room bookshelf. The appeal to a Dorothy Hamill bowl cut–wearing fourth grader? He's FUNNY! It's easy to read SASS. This was a no-bullshit adult man with a perm! Telling it like it is! (I also was a huge fan of columnist Dave Barry at the time, having the humor tastes of a sixty-year-old white man.) Here's one of Richard's HYSTERICAL quizzes!

1. You go to a birthday party where you are served cake and ice cream on the same plate. You decide to eat:
   A. Everything! (Who wants to be rude?)
   B. Just the ice cream or just the cake!
   C. A taste of each and quit

   THE ANSWER IS NONE OF THE ABOVE! BYOF—Bring Your Own Fruit!

He also called out all of us readers, aka "fatties," on our BS. "Do you eat things out of the trash? Girl! Who DOESN'T?" I chuckled balefully to myself, lying on the couch after school in my Girl Scout uniform.

And Richard disses all the other diet programs because this isn't a diet: it's a LIVE-IT PROGRAM. "GOD, HE'S GOOD," I'd think, lounging in my stuffed-animal collection at night, my stomach rumbling with hunger. From the cover, "What are most Americans wearing this year? FAT." OMG. He's the tits! Over the summer preceding fourth grade, I measured my Raisin Bran by the quarter cup, wore weights on my ankles around the house, and lost about seven pounds!

And since this was the early '80s, I got props. The lunch lady asked me, a nine-year-old: "Maria! You look great! How did you do it?"

"RICHARD SIMMONS, Mrs. Mandelhoff, and I'd love to tell you

everything, but I'm squeezing my butt cheeks while not looking in your eyeballs so that you can't see my fear of violently attacking you. Is there any skim milk?"

I also am a sucker for a before-and-after addiction tale. Richard Simmons, who at one point in his life was a very chubby and popular actor in Italy, one day finds a note on his car (presumably in Italian) that reads, "Fat people die young. Please don't die." At that time, Richard Simmons was "morbidly obese." Right then and there, Simmons decided to change. Unfortunately, as he had not yet written his own (more healthy?) diet plan at that time, he starved himself (on fewer than nine hundred calories per day) and lost all of his hair and had to get a lot of plastic surgery for loose skin. I was nine and wanted to lose three pounds. (There had been an ice cream machine at violin camp.)

And this guy had done it! This charming man is TOTALLY IN CONTROL and GETTING LAUGHS!

I love change. Especially dramatic change. So I chose his most restrictive plan of twelve hundred calories a day. I say, go big or go home, or actually go very small and stay home because you're so freaked out by food and your brain distorting your appearance due to malnutrition.

And just like that, I didn't just get thinner and starve, I got depressed, obsessed, and more freaked out than I already was. And undereating is how bulimia starts. After undereating for a few days, when you finally let yourself eat something, it is very difficult to stop eating. I tried to restrict myself, but on "cheat" days I'd start to lose control, finishing a family-size tub of Kemps Chocolate Swirl alongside a jarful of cookies. I'd promise myself that I'd never do it again. Then, a few days later, I'd be off my K rations and back on the couch with bowl after bowl of whatever butter, cinnamon, sugar, flour combo I could throw together in a microwavable dish while watching reruns of *Three's Company*. And since I had started following these chowdowns with intensive bouts of dieting and exercising—jumping on a mini-trampoline or running around the block—I wasn't gaining any weight.

When I hit thirteen and was still doing this stuff, my mom became convinced I was vomiting, because I was eating so much. To her, there was no other way to explain how I wasn't putting on weight. She didn't know I had a DIY 24 Hour Fitness in the furnace room. Looking back, if I had been vomiting, maybe I would have gotten help more quickly. When you vomit, it's a little more obvious, maybe? (Help me out here, former vomiters!) Overexercising can be read as "athletic." However, starving and overexercising can be just as destructive: shin splints; running at night (!) alone (!) when it's fifteen degrees below zero (!); plus the humiliation of constant, foamy, sentient ice-cream farts.

I once told a fellow comic that I had been bulimic.

"For how long?"

"I guess from nine to nineteen?"

"Huh."

"I purged the food with exercise and fasting, though. I couldn't get myself to vomit."

"Oh. Huh. Well, then, isn't *everyone* bulimic?"

Yes, exercise and fasting are tediously common American pastimes, but I maintain that when they stop you from participating in daily life, it's okay to label them as a "dealio." No, I didn't have to be hospitalized for being underweight or blow out my esophagus. So I'm NOT the go-to dramatic speaker on the food-based twelve-step program circuit. But food and weight were a huge part of my life and continue to take up room in my mind that could be used for ethics and wind energy.

I finally called a suicide hotline at the age of twenty, which hooked me up with Overeaters Anonymous, and that helped me stop the binging but not the undereating, isolating, and obsession and so when I was twenty-one, I went through an outpatient program for eating disorders.

And here's a sidebar for anyone who has tried to get mental health assistance and been refused. When I finally got the courage to ask for the insurance-paid help at the University of Minnesota, a family friend who was a DOCTOR—a member of my dad's group practice and also the clinic's corporate insurance-claim investigator—called me at college to question whether I really and truly needed that help.

"You looked fine at Christmas!" Dr. Friend of the Family said. "This is an expensive program for outpatient treatment, and your father's insurance can pay for it, but I just wanted to make sure that it is truly necessary."

I wish I had responded: "Is 'looking fine at Christmas' a diagnosis? Why would anyone want to go through an eating disorder treatment program just for funsies?" I mean, maybe. My husband has a fantasy of going into a beginner's painting class and blowing everyone away with his skill level so that everyone thinks he is a fifty-eight-year-old artistic savant. I guess I could start attending support groups for problems I don't have, like Nicotine Anonymous, and get applause for my fifty-two years of Smobriety.

My aunt Joel Lee had the "more serious" vomiting type of bulimia for twenty-five years, and I remember a screaming fight between her, Mom, and my dad, the subject of which was that my mom was pissed that Joel Lee was vomiting up all the food my mom served. I guess Joel Lee had come for a visit and cleared us out of groceries. That's the only reason I never tried to vomit. *Bamfords don't vomit.* WE do hundreds of weighted squats at midnight, drink chalky Alba "shakes," and down gallons of no-points blueberries. We juice fast while doing wind sprints in the snow, thank you very much.

I don't want to start a war between bulimics, but I think doing calisthenics for four hours after having eaten an entire birthday cake takes a kind of dedication that throat-knucklers just don't have. And yes, I did just throw down. If you've ever been in treatment for an eating disorder, you'll understand it is a competitive sport, even though there are no real winners beyond getting to have a therapist watch you go to the bathroom. Except that one girl who ate so many carrots her face turned orange. That was kind of baller. It's called carotenemia—you eat too many foods with beta-carotene and your skin gets discolored like a superhero. When I eventually did go to outpatient treatment, I wasn't one of the "worst." I guess I should have told my fellow foodies that after I had binged I would pull out hairs from my underarm with a tweezer, just for a refreshing aperitif of trichotillomania. *Plock, fffp, plock, fffp, click, ffffffp, plock.* That's the sound I'd make when I did it, as it's actually a very quiet process. If you've never done it, think pulling out weeds from your yard when the root pops out at the end sometimes. If you've gotten the whole plant, so satisfying! Had I shared that artisanal hair-removal practice with the group, I think that would have gotten me more street cred. But who knows? I also might have been shunned. Even bitches who live on pickles and cocaine have their limits.

When my mom was alive, and 144 pounds heavier, she had museum-quality curatorship of her weight. And even though she stayed around the same size for years—five foot five, 145–165 pounds—Marilyn was always enrolled in some reduction plan that at various times included Diet Center, Bright Line, Richard Simmons, Overeaters Anonymous, Atkins, Ex-Lax, diuretics, Diet Coke, two pots of coffee a day, running, and Pilates.

I had always assumed that my food-focused mother was the source of the family's body dysmorphia. But, when my mom died, we discovered that my dad is the Font of Body Negativity! Over the quarantine, Scott and I put on weight, and my dad, when he noticed—twice—approached Scott, poking him in the belly and saying, "Look at that."

My sister is on a no-sugar, no-flour, no-salt, no-spices (?) cleanse at this time and makes amends to her higher power if she eats the wrong things IN HER DREAMS. I'm not kidding. She writes in a journal to process why she ate DREAM FOOD SHE ATE IN HER DREAMS, I tell you. Here's my current "food plan": I eat a hot-fudge sundae almost every day of the week and when there is no hot fudge, I make do with syrups and heavily moose-tracked ice-cream product. I also eat salad every day. So if I were to open a restaurant, I'd call it "Caesar Creamers."

For me, the bulimic cycles of starving and exercising only got worse without help. The only upside to having an eating disorder for ten years was that the pathological obsession that I was "fat" provided some relief from the even deeper fear that I was just a seemingly inactive but could-be murdering-mammary-mother-manslaughterer.

RECIPE FOR MUG MUFFIN FOR MAXIMUM BINGE EATING

There is no time to think. YOU NEED RELIEF NOW. DO NOT MEASURE. This is to fill the hole inside until you pass out and the frightening scenes in your mind go away for a minute.

1. Pour flour, sugar, a part of an egg, and butter into a mug, in any combination. If this is your third or ninth mug of the day, add some cinnamon. Stir it until it seems like it's something that would bake.
2. Put it in the microwave for two minutes.
3. Add a scoop of ice cream on top and a little paper sack of cocoa mix, stir, and you've got yourself a treat that will make you stop feeling ANYTHING except ill.
4. Repeat six to ten times or until you feel so sick you can't even watch TV or read anymore and have to switch to staring at the pictures in a *Newsweek* and plucking hair out of your arms.
5. Continue this behavior/recipe from the age of nine to nineteen while desperately trying to stop. You cannot stop.

7. Suzuki Violin

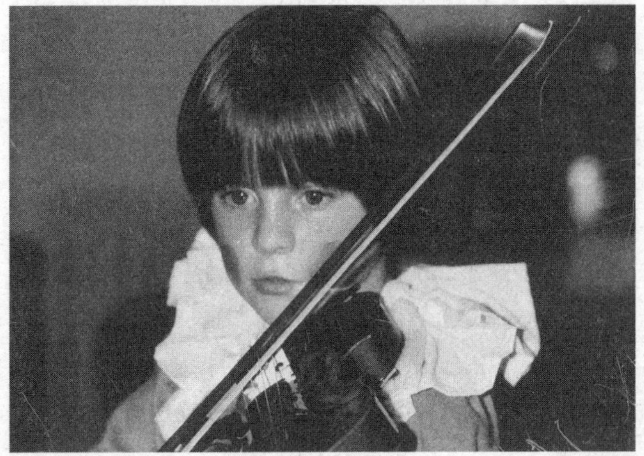

A JESTER TRAPPED

Suzuki violin is a big reason why I've been able to maintain anything like tenacity in any part of life. Suzuki violin is the reason I believe wholeheartedly that if I do anything repeatedly, I will get better at it. The hours put in—not necessarily the passion felt, but the time spent—will get you somewhere, if not everywhere. Discipline in sports, waking up before noon, hosing down your private parts, in whatever tiny, painful increments you can manage, will give you a positive outcome. And that way, when I've had a learning curve to overcome, like learning how to catch the bus in Los Angeles when I'm not able to catch the bus (it's not coming today, it's late, I'm late, it's easier to walk five miles than wait for a bus in LA), I won't just give up, hurling myself chest-first, in shame and resignation, onto the next bus (still not my bus) that comes along.

My experience with Suzuki violin again demonstrates that I HAD EVERYTHING GOING FOR ME. Arts education made a huge difference in my life and continues to do so. As my friend www.jackiekashian.com says, it "kept me off the pole." (This is in no way to suggest that erotic dance isn't a viable life direction as well as a creative, fulfilling, lucrative path that one must be scouted for and deemed worthy of participation in!) The violin also led me to the knowledge that I love EYES ON ME!

I was born in California on a naval base where my dad was stationed as a submariner. My dad then got a dermatology residency in Florida for two years, and we moved to Duluth after he got a job offer at a clinic when I was three. Shortly after our move, my mom asked me, a three-year-old, how I would like to spend my free time. She explained that my choice would cover the next decade of my life, until I turned thirteen, and that there were only two options: dance or violin. The deal was that, whatever I chose, I would have to keep at it, taking weekly classes for ten years. My sister faced a similar ultimatum and went with piano—an instrument I was not offered. Not yet clear on the concepts of either time or commitment, I pondered. Dance vs. violin?

I had done a little jag of tap at the Joyce Torvund School of Dance, which was located in a dusty church rec room. The limited experience I had in the movement arts had involved props and a costume. Since details are not my strong suit, this meant that I performed to the strains of "(How Much Is) That Doggie in the Window?" at my first dance recital without my one mandated prop (a wooden stool I left at home) and without underwear (whoops). It isn't a good feeling to be the only dancing dog in a tutu miming furniture and free-balling it in white tights. From what I could tell by watching the more advanced dance classes, the sartorial responsibilities only increased with time. The four-year-olds were heavily burdened by canes, top hats, and sequined dickeys.

So violin it was! I chose the mysterious unknown over a guaranteed drag. In doing so, I unwittingly volunteered to join the ranks of Suzuki-method violin training, a service division of classical music known for churning out armies of alarmingly small children who can play Vivaldi but who later in life suffer PTSD flashbacks upon hearing the Bach Double Concerto. And there were even more props than there were in dance! In choosing violin, I entered a world of delicate tools that I had to remember and care for: the case (I scuffed it), the rosin (I dropped and cracked it), the bow (*that's horsehair, don't touch it!*), the violin itself (*don't even*), the chin rest (a wobbly combo of foam, wood, and some flannel-type rag to keep from burning a hickey-like callus into your neck), and finally, the unseen presence of repetitive violin music that I was destined to hear so many times the sound of strings effectively affected me like a factory whistle. The idea behind the Suzuki method is simple enough. Shinichi Suzuki, its inventor, had a theory that began with: "Every Japanese child speaks Japanese. It's a very difficult language—and yet babies learn to speak it." Well, the reason Japanese kids learn to speak Japanese is the reason every human being learns their local language: a desperate need to survive and ingratiate oneself in order to gain the unconditional love and affection of caregivers.

Babies (and most adults) will do anything for love. I'm sure if you start out early enough, you can train your kids to be competent in hairdressing, rock climbing, and hog-confinement science by the time they're ten. The question is: Should they be? If you live in Japan, you have to be fluent in Japanese to be a part of society. But let's say I start my two-year-old out on a program of intensive Krav Maga. I'm happy she's learning Krav Maga and my two-year-old is very happy because I'm happy. I'm giving my two-year-old slivers of pepperoni as a reward for her increased Israeli self-defense prowess, and my two-year-old loves slivers of pepperoni. But then my two-year-old becomes three, then four, then five. And as the practice sessions grow longer, even Slim Jims aren't enough to keep her motivated. But my motherly love motivates more than meat! She gets ODDLY GOOD AT KRAV MAGA. Unfortunately, her increasingly complicated knee strikes don't make her popular with others. Yeah, she can do some cool shit, but she hasn't the social skills to connect with her peers, or the greater non-Krav-Maga-practicing world.

Violin performance is a party-stopping, high-kick and cross-body-punch buzzkill at the backyard barbecue. Everyone's impressed (weirded out), but it's not going to make you any pals. Teach your child something useful: how to pay bills online, a way to jazz up Hamburger Helper with cilantro, or a model to maintain relationships not based on your competence at a fairly unpopular skill. Or teach them a second language! Like Japanese!

I know. You think violin will provide your child with structure and a community. Okay. Sure. Just be warned. Your Suzuki-branded teacher is going to ask you to buy Suzuki book one sheet music and, even more deadly, the recordings. "What's book one?" you ask. "Twinkle, Twinkle, Little Star" is the *least* irritating of the tunes, which include the stultifying "Long, Long Ago," as well as the hypnotic enervation of "Go Tell Aunt Rhody (the Old Gray Goose is Dead)." Know that these titles will be seared into your neural pathways. If these songs are being played by a miniature human for whom you are responsible and who represents your devotion as a parent, you may find some satisfaction in their performance. But remember: you also must listen to this recording AS WELL AS TO YOUR CHILD PLAYING THESE SONGS IN PERPETUITY. THAT IS THE WAY OF SUZUKI.

You learn music subconsciously, by ear, like language. Paganini's Caprice No. 24 is NOT in book one, but try playing that on a loop for three hours and note the full-blown panic attack that occurs.

When the baby is just old enough to be propped up, hand her a stuffed cigar box with a ruler shoved lengthwise down the middle and a prop "bow" or stick. Mime repetitively what to do with the box and stick. When they mimic you, applaud, thus creating a lifelong, heroin-grade craving for approval!

As the child learns, reward them with MORE daily practice. And what's the reward for practicing every day? Another practice session called a concert! And because this stuff was written in the '60s, it's a concert for Father! The Father! A Concert for Father! Get a box for the baby to stand on! It is an honor for a baby to stand on a box and play for Papa!

And that is exactly what my mother did. And it worked! Most cults do. I stood on the box many, many times. My first couple of years in Suzuki (ages three to five), Mom bought me whatever I wanted for under a dollar, which was always an ice-cream sandwich from the vending machines in the bowels of the University of Minnesota Duluth student union. On the car ride home, Mom played the aforementioned Suzuki recordings. We never escaped those fucking songs. They played in the car, in the house, and by my bed on a tape recorder as I fell asleep.

My violin teacher was the Grover-voiced Mrs. Dokkep. It was impossible to read Mrs. Dokkep. I could never tell where I stood with her. At the time I started violin, she was in her thirties: short dark hair, ivory skin, with the vocal delivery of Yoda. I thought that she was gentle and patient, but I think I confused those qualities with a STEELY RESOLVE FOR GREATNESS. She would smile slyly when I'd progress on the instrument. But as the years passed and I didn't practice and improve, the cagey smile disappeared.

I didn't understand the use of music as an established psychological torture technique denounced by human-rights activists. I also didn't take in that, after the initial ice-cream-sandwich grooming, I was to be charged with cranking out all these tiresome melodies in public, shoved out on the Suzuki circuit—a pay-your-dues gig that never ended. There were the weeklong summer camp–style recitals on empty college campuses, weekend drives to the big city of Minneapolis to perform en masse, like in a carnival freak show. The love and connection established with my mother during my first two years of lessons (which she attended with me) dried up slowly, imperceptibly, until I was left alone with the lifelong task of practicing, the reward for which was always: more practicing. And not even on a box for Papa. Papa had heard enough. *Papa's listening to Steve Martin's new album.*

The most cultish part of Suzuki was how sealed-off we were from any other types of music. At no time in the fifteen years that I took lessons did we explore anything outside the Suzuki curriculum. I was never asked what kind of music I listened to on my own. Though I'm not sure letting me perform a violin rendition of "Holiday" by Madonna would have hit the spot anyway.

Of course, none of this was Mrs. Dokkep's fault. Going to a Suzuki program and expecting a loose exploration of your artistic tastes is like entering your local comedy club confident that everyone onstage will make you laugh. That's not what the comedy club is for. Suzuki lessons are for learning how to play about a hundred songs in a very specific way, and a comedy club is a restaurant that makes most of its profit on the 150 percent markup on the chicken tenders. It's not about you liking the show—it's about getting ten dollars' profit off every Chris Rock on the Rocks drink sold.

"Hey, Maria, did you find *anything* pleasurable about this enriching luxury experience that your two loving upper-middle-class parents paid a lot of money for?"

I loved the stage. Off the elevated risers, I would cower behind my mom's legs. But once I got in front of everyone with my glossy orange quarter-size JCPenney Stradivarius copy, I felt sunlit and warm. And for predictability, Suzuki recitals—much like comedy shows—are always the same. The producers want to keep you in your seats, so they make sure that the largest part of the audience (those who have come to see the headliner) has to stay through the end. In Suzuki, first up are the insanely good but, let's face it, tiresome advanced students, the few high-schoolers who can actually play a flubless gavotte. Then, progressively, over the course of two hours, the showmanship declines in proportion to the age of the performers—from the book-ten dynamos to a wrenching group of seven-year-olds with piano accompaniment, to what you've been waiting for: BABIES! Most people in the crowd (parents who haven't yet realized the painful journey they are on) are there for the twenty to thirty two-to-four-year-olds simultaneously playing "Twinkle, Twinkle" in a North Korean–style public demonstration of united identical solidarity. When "Twinkle, Twinkle" has been played, as when the check has been dropped at a comedy club, it is almost over. Relieved and sated by their progeny's output, all Suzuki audience members are rewarded with orange drink and sandwich cookies.

Of course, I was young when all of this happened. So to get some accuracy about this period of my life, I did again harass my cancer-ridden mom for her perspective.

"Honey, you loved playing the violin. You *loved* it. I remember you had your first concert and you were so scared that I told you that you didn't have to do it. But you did it and when I asked if you liked it, you said yes! Very enthusiastically. You had a big smile once you got onstage."

So there you go: I am not a trustworthy narrator of my own experience. I may be making stuff up. But it *felt* like that's what happened. I felt all alone, but I was not at all alone and I was loved and maybe even having a great time. And that may still describe me now, despite my whinging.

And just to acknowledge the parents out there, I have listened to hours of small children (and adults!) learning to play the violin, at all levels of development. I see and honor the anguish suffered by those forced to witness it. Their story is no less important than the saga of the players themselves. Please, someone, write a Suzuki parent memoir and let it be at least nine hundred pages with pictures. You have a guaranteed bestseller. May I offer a possible title: *SUZUKI MOM 4 LIFE: I'll Cut a Bitch.*

Looking back, what I did relish—what I delight in to this day—is pleasing others. That first recital was the gateway drug to a lifetime of performance-induced oxytocin. I love attention from groups. Sure, attention from one person is good also, but if I can get a collective positive response for something I've done or not done, my organs light up like a lava lamp.

I do not "embrace the bomb" like some other artists I admire. (Embracing the bomb means that you feel energized by, or appreciate the derision of, a crowd, arms folded, glaring.) I have bombed many times and could bomb again right now—I know where to go! Laugh Factory Saturday night on the Sunset Strip, Vegas, any casino, corporate events, nonprofit fundraisers. But I don't revel in it: despite my best attempts to "ride the wave" of audience dislike of me, I quake and tears fill my eyes.

I go where the love is. And where everyone buys a ticket. No "papering the room," or giving away hundreds of free tickets on a boardwalk or radio station to ensure a full house. I will give you free tickets if you don't have the money and really want to come if you email me at ariamaamfordba@gmail.com. If you can write an email, then you've got skin in the game. But I don't want anyone who doesn't know exactly what they're coming to see coming to see me.

That means: Goodbye, goodbye, "grreat crowd" at a bar in my neighborhood! Hello, Zoom one-on-one show for a stranger I met on Twitter! Hello, whoever is willing to meet me in a Dunkin' Donuts parking lot and laughs at everything I say! Yes, I'm sure my comedy suffers for it. I know

I am limiting my work by keeping myself safe from rejection. But that's okay. Life is short, and it's more fun to spend it where you're welcome.

My mother would send me out to the front lawn to play the violin for our neighbors until the ambushed neighbor audience "really had to go get dinner prepared! Sorry!"

The best thing that Suzuki gave me, besides ice-cream products, was triumph. A sense that I had "won" at something. As in comedy, I would of course find that competition is a losing battle because you're really always "behind" someone even if it's you and your last great performance. But I've always had an embarrassing desire to "smoke" the competition or to SHOW EVERYBODY, which paired perfectly with the growing certainty that this would not be possible. In the Suzuki program, I was over and over again faced with the fact that rumpled, unironed PIERRE BANE, who always forgot his chin-rest foam (me too), had passed me in book eight. And let's not even talk about Andrea Yang or Chip Nosmo. And I'd love to tell you that this music education program was a *Black Swan* backstabbing orchestra pit. It was not. It was an ongoing, low-pressure northern Minnesota–style lesson: just because you're good at something doesn't mean you will enjoy it. It just means that you will be good at it. As I believe it was Dorothy Parker who said, I don't like writing, I like getting money up front.

Imagine something you can do well but that you have no passion for. Let's say, parenting. But you're so good at it that people not only want to see you doing it but hope that you'll get better at it and continue to do it, only with increased focus and determination. And you have to do it all by yourself. Only *you* can do it. So you must continue being a good parent, strive to be better and better at it, but there's no one you can talk to about how much you hate being a parent because that would make you a bad parent and your kids don't have that kind of attention span anyway.

By the age of eight or nine, I was pretty good at violin. Not miraculous good, but good in the way that you look at your short-stack human (or your dog) and say, "If she can do that, I wonder what else she can do? This is fun!" But after the age of six, the violin was just me, alone. I'd head to a closet so no one had to hear me. I'd open my case, set the tomato-shaped kitchen timer for an hour, and start doing scales. Sour, sad scales that I never felt I was getting better at or doing properly because I didn't love it. SLOG SLOG SLOGGING through learning stuff that I would never lose myself in. A little too late in the game, Mrs. Dokkep began asking me for artistry, to RELAX. But along with the part-time eating disorder I was developing, I instead became a grotesque procrastinator—leaving my practicing to the last minute and ghosting Mrs. Dokkep.

I still procrastinate, and I am very familiar with the pattern: the mounting anger at yourself, the longer and longer stretches of time between episodes of taking action. I now know that if I do even thirty seconds on this book or whatever project I'm on, it will help me get rolling.

Had I just been able to pick up my violin for a minute, I would have been better prepared for what turned out to be my final concert. But I refused to pick up the violin. Day after day, week after week leading up to the concert, I refused to touch it. What did I do with my free time? As I mentioned earlier, microwave mug baking followed by exercise.

These days when I procrastinate, I don't binge eat and exercise purge. Instead, I fill shopping carts on the web and then leave them until the clog company sends me a message saying, "Did you forget these three-and-a-half-inch purple suede sandals?"

I get out of procrastination now by calling fifteen people in my twelve-step programs and giving myself motivational stickers for any sign of life. For example, for typing that last sentence, I received from myself a googly-eyed taco. "Taco 'bout a good job!"

To this day, when people learn of my violin-playing past, some non–violin players become surprisingly intense.

"You played the violin for nineteen years? You don't play anymore? Why not? You should! You played for so long!"

Recently, I attended a cookout on a friend's front porch. Their kid is in the Suzuki violin program, and though you can't always tell with kids, the boy seems to be into it, or at least into getting on the box for Papa. The father of this small musician, who doesn't play the violin himself, nagged me, "Maria, come on, you got to get a fiddle and jam."

To me, this is not unlike the suggestion: "Hey, Maria, you know how you were in a toxic relationship for almost twenty years? Why don't you casually reestablish contact? TEXT HIM!"

Believe me, I have tried to reunite with the violin. And I understand the confusion and frustration of seeing someone you love who has hard-won skills that they refuse to use.

The last time I tried playing the violin, I was filming the TV show *Lady Dynamite*, and the writers wanted me to play. I rented a violin from a wonderful small local music store in Sierra Madre for three weeks. I played a short song for the scene. Then I put the violin under my dusty desk in my dusty office and didn't look at it again for three months.

"But Maria! Didn't you just say you had only rented it for three weeks?"

Ah! You ARE reading this book! Yes, I kept putting off returning the violin! In the same way I put off handling it as a younger person! The lovely local music store began calling me. And then I didn't pick up. They left several messages. Criminally, maniacally, I didn't return their calls. I could have easily had an assistant from the TV show I was in return the violin for me. I could and should have told Scott, my husband. He would have happily returned it for me immediately. I didn't tell him. The calls became more urgent. "Uh, hey. We're trying to get ahold of you. We're going to charge you, of course, for the extra time you've been using the instrument, but we'll need your credit card again. Just call us."

I was now, in real time, in slow motion, *stealing the violin*. So: not only did I not play the instrument but I was keeping someone else from playing it and causing a small-business operator undue stress. To make things even more bizarre, upon renting the violin initially, I had begun a giddy conversation with the proprietor about how I'd be interested in lessons. I was a liar and a fraud and now, a felon.

Finally, after several increasingly confused and then deservedly angry voice-mail messages, they sent an email. The store manager informed me that I had now committed grand larceny and they were contacting the LAPD. FINALLY, I told Scott. He sighed and sat next to me while I called the music store and spoke to the understandably enraged owner. I apologized, giving him my credit card to pay for the rental, and then, in a grandiose gesture because I was too ashamed to return the violin in person, I bought the violin itself on my debit card for 750 bucks.

After my payment went through, the music-store owner told me how my attempted crime had affected him in that he couldn't rent out the violin during the time I was harboring it and the amount of anxiety he experienced over the loss of it. He told me he was pissed, irritated, and disappointed with me, as a fellow human being. Yes, yes, and yes! I—of course—listened, agreeing, and acknowledged the rightness of his position. He spoke some more about what a selfish thing I had done. I said it was true and that there were no excuses and never said anything more than "I'm sorry," because at the very least, in being a baloneyhead on the regular, I think I know how to apologize. (LMK if I don't! And I am truly sorry.) Finally, worn out by expressing the most right, righteous anger at a legitimately thoughtless miscreant, he sighed.

"Why didn't you just call us?" he asked.

"I don't know," I said. Because it was the truth. We said goodbye, but I wished that he had hung up on me.

I bet you are wondering: Do I still have the violin?

No. I donated it to a local youth music program.

FIND IT!

You're not good at things. Even if you practice them for hours. IT IS OKAY NOT TO BE GOOD AT THINGS DESPITE ONGOING, TREMENDOUS AMOUNTS OF EFFORT AND DESIRE TO IMPROVE.

1. Spend time with an older dog.
2. Tear one slice of cheese into a bunch of tiny pieces.
3. Now, in a high-, high-pitched voice, yell, "FIND IT!" and throw all the cheese in the air. It will take a while for them to find the cheese. It's supposed to be fun for doggies, but our old pug Max cannot always "FIND IT." No worries. Now YOU can!
4. Sit on the sidewalk curb and "find" the thrown cheese yourself. You ARE good at something. YOU CAN FIND IT.
5. Place the cheese directly into your mouth and that of your older dog. Being good at something is not necessary in order to receive a reward. (If you cannot find the cheese, toss more—with assistance—directly into your mouth and that of your beloved pal.)

8. Dale Carnegie (Winning Friends and Influencing People!)

Jeff Fifield

THE HEADSHOTS CONTINUE!

During my sophomore year of high school, the guidance counselor, Mr. Soren, called my parents to tell them that I was falling asleep through my classes (due to my nocturnal eight-hour Jazzercise shifts) and that maybe something was wrong. This was 1986, so there weren't any eating-disorder treatment programs unless you appeared very Karen Carpenter ill. My mom didn't know what to do (as she already had her own eating disorder). And my dad, like any good dad, invited me along to what he was already doing. Had my poppi been into hunting, I would probably know how to sit for hours in silence in order to terrorize wildlife. But as my dad passed the time with self-improvement, he invited me to take an eighteen-week Dale Carnegie training course on "How to Win Friends and Influence People," held in the basement of the ore boat–shaped public library in downtown Duluth. I said yes, as I had nothing better to do. Dale Carnegie, of course, is the Depression-era American salesman and bestselling author who developed his theories around the same time as Bill Wilson did Alcoholics Anonymous. (They are both faux-Christian "can-do" spiritual leaders of a sort.)

In the carpeted bowels of the library, my dad, myself, and ten small-business-type Duluthians in pressed khakis and reasonable jewelry pulled black metal chairs off stacks and arranged them into a circle, thus beginning what for me has now been forty years of setting up chairs and sitting in circles with strangers, listening to each other talk. Everybody shared why they were enrolled: there was a shy legal assistant wanting to learn how to TALK IN PUBLIC; a tightly wound real estate salesman hoping to make contacts; and the one Black man in Duluth, who drove a taxi and was starting a church. I LOVE A STRANGER WITH A DREAM.

In return for part of the class fee, we each got a copy of Dale Carnegie's *How to Win Friends and Influence People*, which provided very solid if somewhat stilted fill-in-the-blank conversation starters to help you talk to other human beings. The three pieces of advice I remember hold true to this day:

1. Act enthusiastic and you'll BE enthusiastic.
2. The Four C's: don't criticize, condemn, or complain—COMPLIMENT.
3. The sweetest sound to a person's ears, Maria Bamford, is the sound of their own name, Maria Bamford! Maria Bamford!

These simple concepts changed everything for me! I now had a "way." Yes, I still binged and starved and purged via exercise, but my school hours were much improved as I had a social game with attainable "wins." I excel at scripted patterns!

"Hi, Andrew, I love those UMD Bulldogs sweatpants you're wearing, Andrew!"

"Thanks."

Slam dunk and points!

And because these were all northern Minnesota teenagers I was talking to, no one picked up how quite possibly deranged I sounded. I still do this very same setup everywhere I go, but I hope in a more conversational, less robotic, but still manipulative fashion. Just this morning at the coffee shop, I proffered:

"Hi, Emma! I love your earrings."

"Oh, thanks."

"What's Stanley [her cat] doing these days?" (An open-ended question that allows people to expand!)

"Stanley has been tearing up my sweaters and peeing on the bed."

"Oh, Stanley, he's crazy."

(We both laugh.)

Hat trick! Leave with coffee!

I am not an extrovert, and these ploys usually work. They are also how I have made friends and continue to participate in society. Three steps: name, compliment with name, non-yes-or-no question with their name. After that sequence, I'm lost. If someone knows what to do after that besides staring into their phone, let me know. After my opening gambits, if I'm with a stranger in a public place, I'll often give myself a job in order to keep talking to the stranger. Bussing tables, grabbing a towel to wipe down countertops, going to the bathroom and servicing the toilet paper roll.

At sixteen, I adopted this approach 24-7. I talked to my locker-mate

Tina Vergalis for the first time in history. I used it on my friend Kerry, who was high most of the time and didn't seem to notice me saying her name tens of times over the course of an hour while we listened to Led Zeppelin in her Ford Fiesta. I was elated! I can talk to anyone! DALE CARNEGIE WORKS! Of course, speaking to people in memorized dialogue prompts ("Get the customer to say yes, yes, yes!") can be effective, but it lacks that messy, awkward mumbling that I believe is called "authentic human connection." Still, the three-step chitchat was really paying off in the short term!

Feeling inspired, I tried it on a boy I'd had a crush on for YEARS, Wyden Muskrat. Wyden was (and, judging from his very limited internet presence today, still is) the bomb. He is killing it to this day. Soooooo cute. And kind. And a track athlete. And did I mention smart and very funny? Also, track. There is something about track that gets me going, and it is the shorts. He will never read this.

Over several years, I never made it clear to Wyden that I was down for whatevs. But once I start pulling Dale Carnegie everywhere I go—I know the names of everyone in the seventh through twelfth grades, I'm acting enthusiastic, and I'm being enthusiastic—I decide to work this new magic on Wyden. Here is our electric first exchange:

"Hey, Wyden."

"Hey."

"Great job on that speech the other day, Wyden."

"Oh. Uh. Yeah."

I hadn't EVER said hello to him, much less used his name, and I'm sure it was a bit of a shock. That plus the fact that I now did it every day. Every day, I found a way to compliment him. And he would always respond with "yeah" or "thanks." THE INTOXICATING POWER OF A TEMPLATE. After a few weeks of this "Hey, Wyden"–ing, there was no real movement on the romance front. That's when I veered off the normal sales pitch. It was right before Christmas vacation and I decided to just say how I felt, in writing, and then hide over Christmas vacation so I wouldn't have to face him. I wrote, very neatly:

Wyden:
You are handsome, humorous, and interesting.
See you in three weeks,
Maria
218-XXX-XXX0

I placed it in his locker and ran out the door for two weeks of Christmas vacation (pre–internet access). I felt proud (driven?), and though I braced for the possibility of a painful thumbs-down when I returned, it didn't matter! From Dale Carnegie, I had a whole new attitude of a thousand noes just lead you to yes!

And then, that first terrifying day back after holiday break, Wyden said hello to ME. To ME. And then, he CALLED!

SCREAM IN REAL TIME, EVEN NOW.

After several nights of phone calls, Wyden picked me up in his dad's truck and we went to see the movie *Planes, Trains & Automobiles,* and it was the best movie I had ever seen. Thanks to Dale Carnegie, I had no plan after my initial three-pronged scrimmage: calling him by his name, then listening to him and repeating back to him what he'd said exactly. But that seemed to work out—along with making out like crazy. We developed what could be described as a relationship. We fell in love (or at least I did). He was way out of my league—extremely accomplished, level-headed, organized, morally sound, funny—and it would all fall apart two years later due to my mentals. This relationship was such a huge deal for me that I still have dreams about him to this day! Here's to Wyden Muskrat!

And here are the great things he did: Early on in my life, he established that it is possible to be in a romantic relationship where you can both make each other laugh. He was a great letter writer, had beautiful handwriting. And he was really great at sex. He had either lots of experience or some kind of respectful inside information on the female body, because he gave me many wonderful first times! After that, I wouldn't have a good time again until I was thirty-five. (And I didn't know I could just have good sex on my own until I was twenty-four and found a book at a lesbian friend's apartment.)

Wyden gave me the experience of a friend *and* a boyfriend, though I never took advantage of us having a friendship by telling him exactly what was going on (OCD thoughts, eating disorder). Who knows, maybe he would have totally bailed upon hearing about what nightmares were really going on in my gorgeous head. Maybe I dodged a bullet, but as far as I gave him an opportunity to be, he was a good pal.

He was goofy but keeping it together, like Jerry Seinfeld. He got a full-ride scholarship through undergrad AND grad school. And as you know from everything before this sentence, that isn't my style. I eat breakfast from the bottom of my purse, I skim and react to texts, I yell apologies while crashing into your car. I'm fun to watch from a distance in that I give you a sense of superiority.

But it was the longest relationship I'd ever had before Scott—two (2) whole years! And then as we finished high school and went off to college, my bulimia crept back, and the OCD stuff got really bad again. There was a disconnect between who I said I was to Wyden—a marriage-ready go-getter—and who I was, eating pack after pack of mini-donuts, fearful I was a serial killer. I would call him saying I was missing him and yet insist I couldn't change schools (I easily could have and later did change schools). I gained twenty-five pounds and cheated on him with this Super

Gross Person for No Reason at All, and I wish I could blame it on hypomania, but it was just me feeling bad about myself. So in the end, during my sophomore year in college, after many letters back and forth, we broke up via a dorm-hall pay phone (I in Maine, he in Idaho).

"Are you sure you want to break up?" he said. "Because if so, I can never speak to you again." Wyden was and still is very black-and-white. Recently on the FB, I saw that he just opened a pro-life clinic with his wife. (He has blocked me, but I found a workaround and like to check in every couple of years.)

And that was one of many things I loved about him—the rigorous boundaries of good and evil. Once you're out, you're OUT. To this day, forty years later, Wyden doesn't attend our high school reunions because of something his buddies did at his bachelor party (I believe it was invite strippers) thirty-five years ago. I appreciate that kind of exacting clarity. As for myself, because I am not great, I allow a wide berth of behaviors and missteps by my loved ones. Beggars can't be choosers, everybody goes home #nofriendsleftbehind, I don't care what you do as long as we can talk about it later. But I respect separating the righteous wheat from the pointless chaff.

And it was after we broke up that I allowed myself to unreservedly fall apart. The Dale Carnegie chestnut "ACT ENTHUSIASTIC AND YOU'LL BE ENTHUSIASTIC!" is only true if you are a talented actor. Acting is a craft, and with the right lighting, makeup, and CGI, you can be a lithe, fire-breathing dragon. Sometimes you can't "fake it till you make it" (to use a phrase I will learn in my next cult membership!).

A week after breaking up with Wyden, I rang the suicide hotline.

RECIPE FOR WYDEN MUSKRAT BREAK-UP "SHAKE"

It's not a shake.

And you are not a good person. Why can't you be a good person?

1. Locate an attractive-to-you stranger in your dorm, with a fully stocked bar. Have this guy make you a bunch of different drinks over a short period of time.
2. In gratitude for their bartending services, offer sex in thanks. Your partner comments on your cold hands and wonders aloud if you're okay. It's not superb. Wake up. Wonder who you are.
3. Repeat every night until summer break.

9. Overeaters Anonymous

IS THIS THE CURRENT LOGO FOR OVEREATERS ANONYMOUS? WE DON'T KNOW! IF IT'S AN ANONYMOUS SECRET SOCIETY THEN MAYBE I SHOULDN'T SAY, BUT THIS IS WHAT CAME UP WHEN I ENTERED "OVEREATERS ANONYMOUS" INTO THE WORLD WIDE WEB.

Just to remind you, the lightning strike stands for me breaking the rule of anonymity, claiming association in a specific twelve-step group. This act of telling you about it, according to the "traditions," is a big no-no. I don't totally understand it, even after thirty-five years of super-secret enrollment. I have read and reread all the "conference-approved literature." Here is what I *think* are the reasons you're not supposed to say what group you're in publicly:

1. You're making the group about You and You are the Problem?
2. You're a celebrity, dum-dum? Stop bragging?
3. What if you fuck up and lose your shit? It's bad advertising?

4. Your public acknowledgment of participation in a group may prevent someone else from seeking help (as that someone else may hate you)?
5. God has good ideas. Stop asking questions. You don't understand. You're ruining it?
6. You might take over the group, personality-wise, as a "spokesperson" in the public sphere? Like Moses for the Jewish people except with a lot lower stakes?
7. Without arbitrary rules, aren't we just people, sitting in chairs?

Suffice it to say, I'm going to say which groups I've found tons of help in, while also fearing I will be punished either as a social pariah within my support groups or with an actual meteorological strike from somebody's made-up higher power. Back to "breaking my anonymity."

After the break-up, I couldn't leave my dorm room for eating. My roommate, a beautiful Puerto Rican New Jerseyan who made her eyebrows into magnificent arches via hours of artful plucking to a tape of Aretha Franklin hits, asked me, as I climbed up to my top bunk with a full jar of peanut butter, "Don't you have any self-control?"

Uh, no, Natalia. I'm eating peanut butter by the scoop while lying down, almost choking myself, until I pass out. I do not have control of self.

We had a spring break of two weeks and I stayed on campus, ostensibly to volunteer at a sexual-assault hotline. Instead, I called in sick and ate everything that I could get ahold of. In a campus magazine that had been lying on our dorm room floor for months, I read an article about bulimia. It listed the suicide hotline. I called. The woman who answered gave me the number for a free support group called Overeaters Anonymous.

I had been to an Adult Children of Alcoholics Anonymous meeting with my dad a few times when I was fourteen. I knew meetings included prayers, personal stories, and readings from books. I didn't go to a meeting just then, but I planned to go when I got back home to Duluth for the summer. Once I found out about the mere existence of OA from the suicide hotline, I was promptly (and miraculously?) freed from a nine-year pattern of binging/purging and dieting. It was extraordinary and felt slightly supernatural. I think it was probably just hope. Once I began attending meetings in Duluth, I exchanged most of my obsessive food patterns for OA hustle-bustle.

OA (www.OA.org, now in over fifty countries!) was my first twelve-step group—or, as I like to think of it, my first live-action role-playing game.* I started going to meetings every day once I was home from college, mostly in churches and hospitals. It was usually a group of heavier ladies, with the occasional bulimic/anorexic and the even more occasional man. I was terrified I'd "lose my abstinence" (three meals a day, nothing in between, and no dieting/binging/purging). When I think about exactly why twelve-step programs worked for me, I believe it was because:

1. I was desperate, and it was free and the only help available.
2. I was relatively cozy with Judeo-Christian verbiage.
3. I had a positive memory of it. My dad had gone to ACOA and my mom had tried OA, but she stopped because she was worried that "word would get around town." And she's totally right. It does get around town.
4. I could easily change my worldview on a dime (see also Suzuki, Dale Carnegie).
5. Everyone looked like me or my mom.
6. I do not know.

* I promise you it is as compelling and time-consuming as Dungeons and Dragons or dressing up as Captain Underpants for Comic-Con. There are no dice, but there are plenty of plastic poker chips for lengths of abstinence. And you choose your own abstinence like an adventure!

And like they tell you not to do in every twelve-step program, I told everyone about it. I was a huge pain in the arse. I proselytized to my mom and sister. I proudly took four hours to really "devour" a bowl of cereal because I was "eating with gratitude." My family didn't really notice that I had stopped binging—they also may not have thought I had an eating disorder, because in the '80s, as long as you weren't so thin that you had baby hair growing out of your face, you were good to go.

By comparison, my sister and my mom were normal about eating. My mom was preoccupied with food and weight, but it didn't keep her from having a full schedule. She recorded her weight every day for forty years, but she never hid in her room because she "felt" fat. She preferred privacy to openly sharing, and so it's hard to say. Near the end of my ED years, I had total lack of functioning. I really needed to go to meetings and have people to talk to on the phone. However, because these were people without any formal training in eating disorders, the program allowed me to continue being very ritualistic with food—now with added prayer and chewing!

Thirty-two years later, in the last year or so, a dear friend of mine, Yolanda, has gotten into OA. She has swallowed the Big Book whole and is constantly telling me about how much better her life is, being "clean" of sugar and white flour. And I am getting a NutraSweet taste of my own medicine. She just hit me with a few OA classics: "The only thing I have control over is what goes into my mouth and what comes out of my mouth," and "Nothing tastes as good as abstinence feels." All right, Yolanda, calm down. Or maybe I should calm down, as I'm all hopped up on coffee cake from the free hotel breakfast. Sometimes I need to "HALT," kids!*

After all this time, you would think I'd be bored with finding out the

* Don't get too Hungry Angry Lonely or TIRED.

numbers on the scale, but it is forever engrossing to me, like runes or a mood ring or a horoscope, but with far less meaning. I still weigh myself every day. What is the number? Well, as everyone knows, you can't predict it! But I'll tell you one thing: If it's 133, then that means that I have lost control, OH NO OH NO OH NO. And if it's 128, I feel . . . free? Whew. I can finally relax! And yes, of course, I'm fifty-two and hasn't that number changed over the years? It used to be that 128 was BAD and 123 was GOOD. It's totally random and tedious, as all addictions are.

I don't go to many OA meetings now, which is against the rules of fight club. The programs always warn you prophetically about people who "leave the rooms." It's a SLIPPERY SLOPE. ONCE AN ADDICT, ALWAYS AN ADDICT. I see their point. If you fall back into being isolated again, you might resort to your favorite solution of meth-dipped cheese curls. But after I went through an eating disorder treatment program, some of the stuff in OA started to feel punitive, dogmatic, culty. So now I just listen to OA podcasts. In an example of OA fearmongering, when I ended up attending the outpatient treatment program, one of the ED program mandates was that you had to learn to eat everything—that no foods were "bad" or "good"—and I got drop-kicked by my OA sponsor.

I told my OA sponsor—Deb—just to give her a heads-up regarding (and get some support around) the assignment given by my outpatient group. The hospital counselor of the group told me that I had to eat a candy bar and then report back to the group whether or not I had lost my mind. I told Deb. And my sweet-voiced sponsor tossed me like, well, a hot potato (which *is* on the list of abstinent foods, most people's abstinent foods being what you'd expect: no sugar, no white flour). She said, "I WILL DIE BEFORE I EAT SUGAR, I WILL DIE IF I EAT SUGAR, IT'S SLOW SUICIDE!" And she said it with the assertion of someone who is probably doing some other crazy deeds with food on the regs, like bringing "abstinent" cooked oatmeal in Tupperware to a Persian wedding, and a sixty-four-ounce water bottle to a Michelin-starred restaurant. This total rejection by Sugarless Flourless Deb gave me pause. I stopped attending OA as religiously and returned to my non-twelve-step group at the U of MN, with victorious news of tracking and trapping a Snickers bar (sans loss of mind).

But for about two years in OA, I was ALL IN, and now, because of my friend who just joined and is steeped in OA lingo, I know exactly what I sounded like:

Maria! If you fail to plan, plan to fail! (This would work the best in work camp or prison environments where you know what's on the menu every day.)

If you do what you've always done, you'll get what you've always gotten (as applied to . . . fascism?).

Put it in your GOD CAN because GOD CAN. (A GOD CAN is a decoupaged recycled soup can into which one can stuff a written version of one's concerns, like "BRCA1 gene breast cancer," and then, presumably, God will take care of it. It's in His CAN, so of course He CAN!)

Twelve-step programs are rife with mottoes that people repeat solemnly as if rhyming, repetition, and puns are the equivalent of wisdom.

Nothing changes if nothing changes.

Come for the vanity, stay for the sanity.

If you hang around the hardware store, you're going to eventually buy a hammer.

If I may, I'd like to pitch a few more twelve-step slogans to the worldwide fellowship:

Hogs log, get out and jog! (IT HAS TO MAKE SENSE? Oh, okay—I thought wisdom was more about rhyming!)

If I'm not calling, I'm stalling, and that leads to bawling and hauling.

Drugs and ass got me here, but free coffee gave me a ride home.

Booze is dumb and I'm no dummy!

So how do I reconcile my atheist hypocrisy while still attending these groups? My favorite twelve-step slogan is *Take what you want and leave the rest.* This one slogan is how I'm able to rationalize my attendance and constant rule-breaking.

And, thanks to my Diet Coke Can of God, I've been free from binging and dieting for thirty-five years. Howevz, I will not deny eccentric-eater status. Whenever I can, I have ice cream for breakfast, served in a mug with a scoop of chilled peanut butter in the middle. Our family (Scott and I) cannot seem to handle having cookies in the house. If we have cookies in the house, those cookies become dinner, and thirty minutes after dinner, in a sugar crash, we are both in tears, rolling and writhing on the front lawn. As far as my eating style, I am also a little disgusting. I love my fingers and how agile they are at getting things in my mouth as quickly as possible—so much faster than a fork! Scott sometimes points at my face and says, "You've got something. . . ." Of course I have things on my face. That's how they get close to my mouth. My messy face breaks into a slow and bashful smile.

GAS STATION BENEFIT BANQUET FOR TWO

1. Stop at any gas station, by car or on foot.
2. Open the door to the "mart." There, you will find glorious, unmined "high-value treats," as they are known in the dog-training business. These are rare, not-good-for-you bits and chips with which you can convince yourself to pay attention or learn something.
3. Grab your favorite tall-boy version of soda. CHECK THE EXPIRATION DATE.
4. Select a strange new type of untested PowerBar or giant cookie. AGAIN, CHECK THE EXPIRATION DATE.
5. Pay the human being behind the bulletproof glass who is at work, and if you have it, ask for twenty dollars cash on top of your purchase or use the sun-bleached ATM to get out some cash.
6. Now—and this is the most difficult part but also the most rewarding—GIVE THE TWENTY DOLLARS to the stranger working the register. Let a moment pass for them to understand the twenty dollars is now theirs. In an emotional display, pop open your tall boy and yell, "Here's to YOU, the worker!"
7. (If you don't have the cash, instead purchase an alcoholic beverage that includes both beer and tequila, leave the drink on the counter as a gift, and amp up the volume of your pronouncement from a cheery 7 to a militant 10.)

PART II

Cult Following: The Cult of Fame

10. Showbiz! The Cult! *The Artist's Way*!

ON MY (ARTIST'S) WAY!

Oh my. The busker with upper-class roots: my five-year-old Corolla (paint/bumper stickers my own) is courtesy of Marilyn and Joel Bamford (add in the LAURA ASHLEY designer dress I'm wearing with otherwise thrifted baseball hat, dead man's sweater, and high-tops with men's basketball socks). This is a post-performance begging shift with my violin in DT Minneapolis. I believe the blocked sticker reads WOMEN POWER and the blurry one is illegible, but let's just assume I have completely sold out on these values long before the stickers were torn off the vehicle (in a DT Los Angeles parking lot where I was temping in commercial real estate). I had it repainted a sedate navy blue at Earl Scheib North Hollywood when I became a health-insured cog in the capitalist machine.

I LOVE SHOW BUSINESS AND ALL OF ITS CEREMONIES! But it's like a friend who is an alcoholic. Your beloved friend drinks a ton, and they are sometimes very drunk. It can be fun if they're coherent and being claustrophobically supportive while spitting in your face. But once in a while my buddy showbiz is in a blackout—a little mean, teary-eyed, and wanting to borrow money. I still love my hard-partying comrade. I just can't act surprised that my friend or showbiz doesn't know me five minutes after telling me I'm a genius they want to marry. Showbiz, like your best friend after eight shots of tequila, is out of its mind! On the regular, showbiz tries to refuse me entry to the theater where my name is on the marquee until I hold a driver's license up to the poster of my face outside.

At twenty-three, I had graduated and was doing stand-up and performance art (in the very same act) in Minneapolis. By then, I'd been in Overeaters Anonymous for a couple of years, and the meetings had lost the freshness of a brand-new philosophy. I was eating normally and I was also now medicated for depression via the ED outpatient program doctor. I didn't "feel" Prozac's effects directly, but thanks to the drug in combination with the outpatient group, I began having more fun, trying stand-up and having a larger view of the world, which included more than just the Serenity Prayer with my eyes closed.

I started to feel better with only a small side of weep. (I didn't realize at the time that most people don't hard-cry every day.) My biggest practical problem was that I didn't earn enough money to live on, but I found a budget-conscious lifestyle renting from hippies and then not paying rent for a year while occasionally working at a pizza restaurant and begging my codependent parents for money.

I was feeling aimless. I had gotten some books from my local library: *Feel the Fear and Do It Anyway* by Susan Jeffers, *Creative Visualization* by Shakti Gawain. I was part of an improv group called the "Wizards of Odd." I had a mailing list (the paper kind) for anyone who was willing to sign up to receive my cut-and-pasted-up postcards. That was an idea I took from *Guerilla Marketing,* another FREE library book. But I felt a little uncertain as to what to do next.

I needed a new WAY! At around that time, a friend, mentor, and fellow comedian who wrote for TV, Frank Conniff, gave me a copy of *The Artist's Way.* The author, Julia Cameron, had started writing it as a class handout for community colleges in New York City. It turned into a worldwide bestseller. It's got a passel of spiritual language, but I believed in God at the time. And it gave me the confidence to say what I already was—a comedian!—and to recognize what that might mean, in terms of what I wanted to happen in my life professionally!

Though Julia Cameron suggests going through the exercises of the book with other people, I knew how sensitive I was about my creative work: I crumple after the most benign criticism of "Not my cup of tea" (two stars, Audible review no. 112, I see you). I went through the whole book of exercises by myself. Twice.

The reason I had faith in the process was because I still had an imaginary friend in the spirit world. Until I was around thirty-something, I believed in some benevolent personal deity. Belief in God was closely tied for me to hypomania—the belief that I was on a divine path. This bled easily into the belief that some all-knowing being gave a taint about me being a comedian. As far as I can tell thirty years later, this cannot possibly be true.

My atheism slowly developed alongside the growing realization (which dawned on me while I was experiencing the highs and lows of LA) that the world is abominably unfair AND filled with love? I'd eventually come to the conclusion that "God" could very possibly be a combination of privileged luck of the draw and an overuse of caffeine. Now I only believe in humanity and the human ability to do good, but at the time of my *Artist's Way* devotion, the "God" idea got me through twelve chapters of filling in sentences like "My favorite thing to do as a child was _________________."

(The answer was "piggyback rides." Scott does give me piggyback rides in our pool, which renders me weightless. All things are possible with a pool.)

Via the book's recommendation to do positive affirmations to fight negative thoughts like "I am a hosebeast made of hoses and beast," I began saying to myself, ten times a day, "I am one of the top ten comedians in the United States." I limited myself to one country. I didn't want to learn French, Arabic, or Chinese. As a result of completing the workbook sections, I wrote and performed a comedic one-person show (that would years later become a successful web series called *The Maria Bamford Show*) and produced it over and over again in Minneapolis, anywhere anyone would let me. I wrote and performed it because the book said to do it. There was no real interest from the outside world about these activities beyond a good-natured "Good for you!" or, more commonly, "Oh," but due to the support of Cameron's book as well as to the fuzzy future fantasy of Making My Dream Come True, I had a fiery false engine pushing me forward with no need for external validation.

AND WITH IT, THE PROMOTION BEGINS!

City Pages April 94

ArtCetera

Wham, Bamford

Anyone who has ever wrestled with a sibling knows the exquisite sensation of tickle torture. The true master of the technique knows its dual purpose: either to induce tears or to prevent them after a particularly fierce blow to the solar plexus. Either way, it is an insidious tool: laughter and pain are uneasy companions. But for Maria Bamford, whose *Sex and Violins* runs through April 17 at Bryant Lake Bowl, joy and hurt are inseparable.

In her one-woman show, Bamford alternately pushes and drags you through a schizophrenic account of her personal, sexual, and bulimial history, pausing only for the laugh that seems unseemly a moment later. Between bits of stand-up and throw-up humor, Bamford races through character pieces so quickly she appears to be exorcising demons.

But while Bamford's material gets dark, her manner never does. With the help of her violin, "Roberta," Bamford pulls the mood around with little ditties that commemorate relationships and the glory of menses.

Bamford is wonderfully bizarre on stage, capturing the perfect pose of each of her characters: cheerleader, mother, and her own limping, introverted self.

—Anne Schindler

The Artist's Way helped me have the audacity to try things that I probably wouldn't have considered before. I was an "actor," I was a "comedian." I auditioned for parts I saw in the paper; I signed up with a commercial acting agency (a scam) that profited off clients they represented as "everyday models"—which is not a real thing. (They tell you, "You have an everyman look," and then charge $1,500 for headshots.) I performed my violin/character-based show that may or may not have been comedy at coffee shops at 5 p.m. And after two years of performing around the Twin Cities, I applied for a job as a costumed character for a live-show version of *Star Trek* at the Mall of America. I LOVED AUDITIONS BEFORE MOVING TO LA!

Auditions in high school had only eight people! There were only eight parts! I got a part! Followed by show, party, and friendships! We were all superstars! Apple pie à la mode at Perkins for everyone! Auditions in college were a little more competitive, but you still got lines! Also followed by show, party, friendships! Keg party for everyone! No, YOU were great!

Auditions in Minneapolis! Yes, there are a few more people auditioning! These people are adult professionals! Some of these actors have "booked" the role of Gedney, the Minnesota pickle, before and are returnees! You are up against SHOO-INS who know how to run in a pickle suit when it's 110 degrees and you've got to get back to your car without having people "lose the mystique" behind Gedney by seeing you stuffing the pickle costume in the hatchback of your Comet! I GET A CALLBACK! But I *turn down the pickle job* due to fear for my safety (two former pickles—both of whom were men over six feet tall—said it was a regular thing to be chased and punched). I'M TURNING DOWN JOBS! I'm an IN-DEMAND PICKLE!

I had never been turned away from the arts, a benefit of working in very small markets. Sure, there'd been some looking away or cold stares when I turned on a microphone in an otherwise peaceful coffeehouse, but this was Minnesota—the state of deflected confrontation (unless you have any melanin in your skin, in which case it's racist AF). I had never been disappointed. I always got A part if not THE part. And I felt proud auditioning for what would be my first paid show-business gig for PARAMOUNT (Parks). I went for it, doing my impersonation of Andrew Dice Clay's dick joke but from a feminine perspective, with me screaming, "HE WAS SUCKING ON MY BOX!" (Please listen to my Audible book to hear this performance in full.) I had just turned down Gedney: I was doing Paramount a favor!

And I was hired! By a weary-looking bald Black man named Stan. I'm not sure why he took me, but I am forever in Stan's debt. For the aforementioned Big Break Star Trek Job, I would be paid more than I had ever been. Six hundred dollars a week! My dream of being a comedic actor had come true! I was playing the part of a Major Lelanka (my choice) of the planet Bajor in my very tight costume, giant breasts (a padded bra to make me a galactic C cup), and alien nose applied with spirit gum. SEE PHOTO ON PAGE 129.

This job was not really acting so much as it was a full-time improv game to get people to take pictures with you for an extra twenty dollars as a part of a paid STAR TREK EXPERIENCE. What I didn't tell Stan is that I am VERY SHY. I also don't like to bother people. I am NOT GOOD with people. Performers can be shy. Stop being shocked, morning radio hosts. Stage performance is a controlled environment in which to communicate one's limited worldview without interruption. That's my wheelhouse: one-way speechifying. Either I pontificate or I am a silent witness. I'm onstage amplified and lit or I'm in a dark corner eating seasoned curly fries alone. This job as a jovial roving space clown was very much outside my comfort zone. Not only would I be chewing the fat with the monstrous public, I'd have to blather in character to my fellow costumed colleagues: a Vulcan, a Klingon, and a Ferengi. As *The Artist's Way* promises, you will sometimes fear your own success! Don't make a creative U-turn! You said you wanted to be an ACTOR! THIS WAS ON YOUR VISION BOARD!

During each shift of the starship *Enterprise*, people who might have been interested in taking pictures with us were extremely disappointed by our lack of knowledge about the *Deep Space Nine* franchise story lines.

STAR TREK FAN: Remember when [NAME I DON'T RECOGNIZE] was lost in [PLACE I HAVEN'T HAD THE WORK ETHIC TO RESEARCH]?

ME [*in a pseudo-British(?) dialect*]: Ah yes! You speak of the television series made about my people. That is not my true history, which is one of tragedy and genocide, but is something called, I think you call it FICTION in your world. I know nothing of this television series, but tell me more. Would you like a photo of me for use in what you humans call your SCRAP booklets?

Wouldn't it have been great had I buckled down and done homework on Star Trek in order to play the character well? Yes. Oh well. It's a bit of a pattern I have. It's called "phoning it in," or "trying to get away with the least possible amount of effort." It's my calling card. But I made it through the four-hour shifts despite waves of nauseating social anxiety. Did I actually hate this acting work that I had claimed to want? Whoops. I must have done a reasonably professional performance because Stan said if I moved to LA I could do more of these insanely well-paying gigs at Jack in the Box restaurant promotions and close-to-unattended mall events all over central and southern California.

One way I had gotten myself to show up for work at the Mall of America in Minneapolis was to start a very exciting backstage make-out relationship with a traveling Vulcan (getting green makeup all over my face). The Vulcan was a chain-smoking heavy drinker named Nate who lived on the beach in Venice, California, but was in space for a few months to pay the bills. This is also a thing I do: workplace romance as distraction from fear. Via the propellant of our passion, I made it through the two months of shows. And shout-out to Nate: the fantasy of him being a long-term boyfriend then gave me the audacity to drive my totaled Corolla ("Do not drive this," said the mechanic) two thousand miles in fits and starts (it broke down three times) across the Rocky Mountains.

Forgetting about the presence of the Rocky Mountains between Minnesota and California was a metaphor I would take in later. Yes, your dreams might come true, but there are going to be these massive obstacles that anyone could have told you about, historically documented peaks to climb that were clearly marked on a map. Moving to California might be described by most rational people as "a good time to get some feedback before making a more well-thought-out plan." Unfortunately, for me, as a twelve-step-higher-power-head with light mania, it was what I called a GOD SHOT!

As soon as I even had the idea to move, I packed everything up in my squished-on-four-sides Toyota Corolla, gave away a futon, and secured the promise of a bed I could rent for two weeks through a comedian friend of a friend who lived in a place called Palms. I spoke excitedly with my boozy bf chimney Vulcan (scaring him enough to dump me as soon as I breached LA County) and made a very insecure agreement with a gay Klingon from Wisconsin about being roommates. I was being led! By

Goddess! And just as La God planned, I got to LA, rented a place with my fellow Trekker, and soon found there wasn't enough Star Trek work to pay the rent! But don't worry! I bailed on the Klingon and found a cheaper place in Koreatown that I couldn't afford either!

Then the entire division of Paramount Parks dissolved and Stan disappeared!

I got a job at Crown Books and got fired for stealing. I wasn't stealing. I was just incompetent. I didn't know how to do returns on the cash register and didn't want to ask. It was after Christmas and I gave people their money back without recording it via buttons on the machine. The manager at Crown Books—after firing me—wanted to rehire me when I told her I was just too scared to ask how to do returns properly, but I like a clean break. I'd moved to Koreatown. I quickly got a job at a cafe, which began behind the counter, but I was too slow and they moved me to the back of the bakery, loading trucks. Then I ran out of money and ran out of food, but I AM ONE OF THE TOP TEN COMEDIANS IN THE UNITED STATES! Maybe I need to learn HOW MATH WORKS.

The Artist's Way, for good or for ill, gave me the permission and inspiration to go do exactly what I wanted to do without anyone (but the now elderly and probably exhausted Julia Cameron) for support. Turns out Julia C. is also bipolar. That would have been good to know.

Her book is filled with exercises I found helpful that can be filled out sincerely or with irony and humor. You transform your critical BLURTS to loving AFFIRMATIVES. You write out what your head tells you and then make up the exact opposite and post it where you can see it on your ceiling over your bed.

Here are my current BLURTS:

- I am a hog-pig. I hog-pig everything. I am not even an intelligent hog-pig wearing tailored dresses with an Instagram following like the pig in Canada named Esther (the Wonder Pig).
- My work is facile. I am shellfish and selfish. Everyone/everything could live better without me. I am a withered pouch of low blood pressure in a deteriorating caul of papery skin covered in thick black arm hair.
- I am a sluice of spittoon effluvia.

Now, let's turn it around!
Here are my AFFIRMATIVES!

- I am a hen. I sit on eggs to warm them. People like my eggs when I pop one out on an unpredictable schedule that is hypnotic.

- My work builds low-income communities from healthy spine meridian fascia. Like Mother Earth, I give and give and give. Nothing in this world can survive without my jokes-yolks.
- I am a brilliant, defined tropical fruit Jell-O mold that feeds children at risk.

I've since tried to recapture the original epiphanous feelings I got when I first read *The Artist's Way*, but I've always got to fool my head with fresh dogmatic catchphrases, and therefore, ON TO THE NEXT CULT!

RECIPE FOR THE ARTIST'S WAY

1. Find something that might be edible.
2. There's that block of tofu you never did anything with.
3. Put it in the oven.
4. Set the oven for 475 degrees.
5. Do not watch it.
6. When the smoke alarm goes off, take a look.
7. See what's happened.
8. YOU ARE NOW IN FLOW.

11. Debtors Anonymous!

Debtors Anonymous (www.debtorsanonymous.org) is as huge in LA, NY, London, and Paris as it is inordinately expensive to live in those cities. I learned about Debtors Anonymous because my Overeaters Anonymous sponsor, Beth, told me it might help. I was living in a cockroach-infested apartment in Koreatown where the landlord allegedly accepted sex for rent; I had accrued five thousand dollars in medical debt, had no way to pay rent, and was living on a steady diet of two-day-old croissants from my bakery job and generic PB in a quart jar from a bulk store called Smart & Final. I will tell you of my DA journey in the classic structure of a twelve-step share, in which you say what it was like, what happened, and what it is like now.

WHAT IT WAS LIKE

My first memory of money is saving up twenty dollars of allowance at the age of eight and putting it all in a church collection plate. I had been hoping that there was a "Give Cam" of some kind that would record and televise my good deed: I wanted to be recognized (at the very least by my father sitting beside me) as an excellent human. As I would find with ever-larger donations, no one is watching the Give Cam! When I was thirty-seven and starting to get paid more, I gave $50K to a charitable organization. There was no trophy, no crown of flowers, not even a horn blast. There was just a generic thank-you letter telling me to keep it for my IRS records and then a phone call to see if I wanted to give more money. Fair enough! They are busy using that $50K to help people get their basic needs met! I am an asshat!

As far as financial stability in childhood goes, aside from my mom panicking once every five years that we were "broke," we lived, as I understand now, very large. Duluth is a beautiful city with a billion amenities, good public school funding, and three colleges. My dad was a physician and my mom had a college degree (and later went for an MSW after my sister and I both left the house).

In a family of high-achieving perfectionists, one of my fantasies was to achieve eminence in something. I recognize greatness. As I write this right now, the baristas at this coffee shop are KILLING it—twenty people in line and they are distributing the orders with verve, calm before a frankly merciless audience. Unfortunately, people are bringing their maximum 24-7 all over the world to no applause. Everyone deserves a raise. And, I would argue, they deserve a raise especially if they are BAD at what they do. The pain of not being good at your job while continuing to do that job could be considered OT.

When I don't succeed the first one to three times in being good at something, I fold. But sometimes you can't get fired, despite your best efforts (or lack of them).

My first job was mowing the lawn and cleaning the house—otherwise known as contributing to my family. My second job was working at JCPenney in the lingerie department. This lasted only until it became clear that I had no real understanding of breasts and the fitting of them. I was moved to the wedding registry department, where I knew even less.

Later, to supplement my JCPenney job (that I was doing so poorly at), I got a job waitressing poorly at the one Mexican restaurant in town, Hacienda del Sol. If five tables sat down all at once on the outside patio, my station, I'd hide in the shack where the SodaStreams were kept until at least two tables left. The third job I got that year required me to sell furniture at a chain store called This End Up. The furniture was very sturdy, made out of shipping crates and perfect for group homes, halfway houses, and rambunctious families of six with dogs. It wasn't exactly attractive. In two full years of working there, I only sold two pillows and one bunk bed, but that's because the couple was adamant about wanting to buy them. My boss, a lovely lady named Laura, once took me to task, saying that a security guard she knew in the mall told her I was just eating my whole shift. Yes! I was. This was early recovery days in OA, and it took me six hours to consume two pieces of wheat bread with three squares of honey ham.

The great thing about spending so much time being a horrendous employee is that now I can spot a fellow sufferer easily. When the young lady running the Hampton Inn lobby doesn't know (and does not care) why the WiFi isn't working—

FRONT DESK WORKER SHAYNA [*laughing*]: I know, right? I can't get ANY service. Crazy!

SHAYNA AND ME: [*Laughs!*]

ME: Oh well!

There's probably a solution to the nonworking WiFi, but I get it, Shayna. Let it ride.

And yes, you can slide by doing a not-great job, especially in Minnesota. Customers and colleagues will be disappointed, but it is unlikely that they will say anything to your face. Los Angeles has higher expectations (a tighter, more skilled job market, millions of people who know how to show up, how to work, and how to be pleasant while doing that work).

Los Angeles food service is at professional-sports level. Each citizen of LA—whether you are ordering Cheetos from a food truck or vegan caviar from a golden vitrine—*everyone* in LA County has the right to request sides, on the side of the side, less of this, more of that, and FAST. *People on the coasts send food back.* These big-city types have had the best and they don't have TIME. They may have endless patience in the wait for their dreams to come true, but not for waiting more than three minutes on a triple-shot cappuccino, "bone dry." Up until my move to California, it had never occurred to me to speak up if I got half-frozen chicken tenders. They're cooked at the factory, right? If some kid in the kitchen is having a bad day at work, why make it worse by sending back what they so nicely slid out for me with a piece of their pretty, long brown hair on a plate?

After my Space Travel stopped, I needed money. I tried to get back into food service with one (1) graveyard shift at a twenty-four-hour deli in Century City, but upon greeting a table full of Westside teens with orders including essay-length drink requests and single maraschino cherries on the side, I quit. From there, I applied to a coffee shop in the Little Ethiopia/Fairfax district of LA, and my anxious presence was almost immediately recognized as what you might call "unabled." But the bakery owners didn't fire me. They allowed me to stay on working after hours, in the back, packaging brownies, croissants, and lemon bars for this new thing called Starbucks. It was me and five young strong guys from Honduras and El Salvador, loading trucks. I knew enough Spanish to understand that they had a nickname for me, Cara de Cebolla, which means "Onion Face." Ha-ha!

One of the guys at the coffee shop, whom I made friends with, was named Bernicio. He was going to community college and took two buses to get to this bakery for work at night. One night, Bernicio and I were spanglishing and he asked, "So, wait, you have a college degree?"

"Yes."

"And you're working here?"

"Yes."

"*Por QUÉ???*" (Why?)

Bernicio was pissed at me for not taking advantage of every advantage I had been given, which included every advantage. And he was correct.

I was an idiot.

At the same time that I was working at the bakery, my car was falling apart and I couldn't pay my rent to the pimplord. On top of that, in an effort to have a good time, I got a pretty nasty STD from a fellow space traveler. Always wear a condom with a Ferengi, am I right, fellow aliens?

My cooch was in a rough state. After much shame and putting off, I went to Planned Parenthood to take care of the vag traj. This was the PP on Vermont and Hollywood Boulevard. I had assumed they'd be nonchalant. They had seen their share of conditions. But upon checking the engine, my female doctor disgustedly shuddered. "How did you let this get so bad?" she asked. "Why didn't you come in earlier? You are educated!" Well, then. My apologies. She prescribed an antibiotic. This drug, erythromycin, taken when I got back to my bug-filled, possibly-sex-bartered apartment, gave me a severe allergic reaction: difficulty breathing, dizziness, and an inability to keep my tongue inside my mouth.

I crawled over to knock on some teen runaways' apartment door and they thought I had OD'd. They called 911, and an ambulance took me to the ER. This cost around five thousand dollars, split among four separate health-care providers, all of whom invoiced me immediately. The truck-loading work I was doing didn't pay enough to cover even rent and groceries, much less medical debt. The creditors started calling every day. Then I got mugged (my purse taken), robbed (my already maxed-out AmEx number taken), and I ran out of the 40 mg per day of Prozac I was supposed to be taking. In a panic to get meds, I almost got myself hospitalized at County when I said I was suicidal (I had to admit to the doctor I'd waited six hours to see that I was just desperate to get meds, and she gave me a script for eight days' worth of Prozac).

The obvious question at this point was, why not ask your upper-middle-class parents for cash? Oh! I already had! Many times! And Marilyn and Joel had bailed me out! This practice ended when I moved to LA. When I told my mother, in tears, of my most recent fiduciary emergency, Marilyn responded with, "No." In retrospect, that refusal was the most loving thing someone had ever done for me. "Honey, we support you emotionally but not financially. We know you can do this." If my mom hadn't stopped enabling my unsustainable lifestyle, I never would have found any willingness to get the help of a new cult!

WHAT HAPPENED

GOD SHOT! The first Debtors Anonymous meeting I went to was within walking distance of my insect-packed pied-à-terre.

One good thing about me is that I will follow directions once they are given to me. I will not ask how to do anything, but if you tell me how to do it, I will do it. The group told me to get a sponsor and a "PRG," or Pressure Relief Group. I got a sponsor right away (Mindy), and scheduled a PRG (Mindy and Phil). What is a PRG? It's a self-propelled intervention on your current situation. It's brought about on your own volition (you have to ask two people of your choosing). There is info online on how to do it, but essentially:

Everybody says a prayer (I do deep breathing and think of old pugs).

The person (me) who has asked for the PRG writes down whatever they want out of the meeting. For example, "What to do with the guy who says he's going to kill me if I don't give him 25K by midnight," or, "How to send people all those magnets I owe them from a three-year-old board-game Kickstarter I never followed through on." Right now, I might want to have a PRG on how to finish this book by the deadline next Monday (it's Thursday and I won't).

Then the pressure relief–ees brainstorm some possibly helpful actions to take that you might not have thought of. The PRG people tell you their stories and what has helped. You all have some much-needed laughs! Hopefully, you've picked someone in the group who has experience arbitrating payment plans with la Cosa Nostra or someone who's sent out mass-mail apologies via Sticker Mule. My own PRG for this book might say, "Have you thought about asking for another week to finish?" No, I haven't, but now that you've said that, I will give that a shot and the editor will say it's fine and I'll have an immediate relaxation response.

My first PRG was set at Phil's house. Both Mindy and Phil, without knowing me from Bill W. (cult joke, ha-ha!), spent two full hours with me, coming up with ways that I could improve my situation in ways I hadn't thought of. They also laughed at my jokes. Weeks later, Mindy listened to my step work, which if you haven't done it is like a slow-burn confession and then, hopefully, a transformation of lifelong self-sabotaging behavior into something slightly less dysfunctional. Depending on how old you are or how pathologically, compulsively thorough, the step process can take anywhere from a minute on a cocktail napkin to a lifetime on graph paper.

They (THE PRG! Otherwise known as people willing to help) suggested to me in 1995 the following actions:

1. Call everyone you know to see if you can rent a room. Ask if you can do a payment plan for the first few months.
2. Ask God, or Yoda, or your pet lizard, or *Miss Piggy* for the willingness to earn two thousand dollars a month, which was the amount we determined I would need in order to pay for rent, food, health care, clothing, and some kind of debt repayment in 1995 Los Angeles. (I had never in my life earned more than nine thousand dollars a year.)
3. GET A JOB, any JOB. You can type, Maria, and you have a BA in English. Sign up with five temp agencies. Call them as soon as they open, while fully dressed and ready to go, and say, "Good morning! My name is Maria and I'm available for work!" You do not have to "mean it." You can fall asleep in those work clothes right after, but you MUST CALL EVERY DAY AS SOON AS THEY OPEN and, no matter how irritated they sound, say, "Hi, I'm available for work!" I did this so regularly (and I took to sleeping with my shoes and clothes on) that twenty-five years later, when my friend Pat used my name as a reference at the AppleOne agency, they still knew me. "We remember Maria. She would do ANYTHING!" I signed up with AppleOne, Pro Staff, People Power, Accent, and one more company whose name escapes me but let's call it "Meat in a Seat."
4. Take the CBEST (California Basic Educational Skills Test) for emergency certification and substitute teaching. I did do

this, but I was so frightened of every grade level that even though I got certified and read a whole nonfiction book about substitute teaching, I could not get myself to sub.

5. Type out form letters for all creditors. Leave the space for your current payment blank. Either send just the letter acknowledging the debt, or send the letter and a payment, but NO MORE THAN TWO DOLLARS (or zero if you don't have it) every month. In the letter, tell them not to contact you by phone. (Note: this works for everything but the IRS, cousins, friends, the Mob, and student loans.)
6. Go to Disneyland.

I did everything they told me to except for number 6, because I am not going to Disneyland. I called everyone I knew and finally found a comedian friend of a comedian friend who had an extra room in Glendale that she said she would rent to me for three hundred dollars a month. After we talked and she agreed to let me move in, I had the embarrassing task of letting her know I had absolutely no money to move in and I'd need to do a payment plan for that three hundred dollars over the course of three months. She let me be her roommate anyway. Shout-out to Steph Hoff!

I did what the PRG told me: I sent out letters to all the creditors and they stopped calling! Instead, they began sending me all-caps form letters from MR. BLACK or MR. PINK saying that WE ARE NOW TAKING LEGAL ACTION. They NEVER TOOK LEGAL ACTION. They did, however, send me legal threats for a very long time. Eventually, I was able to pay my debts off in full. And, as with all financial transactions, no marble statue was carved to commemorate this. After taking the suggestions of the PRG, I felt considerably better. And now not only did I have Mindy and Phil to call when I was struggling, I had a group of about seventy-five people every Saturday morning who would laugh when I said I didn't want to go to work!

Of course you don't want to work! BWA-HAHAHAHAAHAHAAAH! This is the great thing about twelve-step support groups. You can share the grossest elements of your personal failings and all you will hear is peals of joyous recognition to the rafters of whatever Zoom breakout room you're in.

And thank Allah for that, because I was resistant to anything that I didn't know how to do . . . which was everything. But my PRG and everybody in the group said, "Earn or burn!"™ And I did, little by little, earn more and more with constant cheerleading from a group of strangers. Having signed up at the temp agencies, I contacted everyone I knew to say that if they needed something done for money, I was available. I painted my friend Peter Spruyt's fence (poorly), destroying his rosebushes. I resentfully and poorly cleaned apartments. I resentfully and poorly decluttered. I took every job the temp agencies offered—factory work, stuffing envelopes, being an audience member for TV shows. The only time I turned down a job was when they asked if I'd be okay coming to an unmarked warehouse at 5 a.m. to work with knives. It turned out to be making salads for the airport, and maybe I missed out, but I'm not great with sharp things.

The important thing was that the support of the group got me out of my fears of WHAT TO DO? They advised me to pawn something if I needed cash (I got twenty bucks for a VHS player so I could buy gas) and to be willing, one day at a time, to "be of service." Those phrases—"one day at a time" and "be of service"—will be familiar to anyone who's sat briefly in a twelve-step meeting. The idea of "one day at a time" is that you can do pretty much anything for one day. You can't promise you'll keep it up for a lifetime. Or in my case, for one nanosecond, since I always want to escape a job as soon as I get there.

The idea is to get you to stop obsessing about what you're "really" supposed to be doing. What's in front of you? What isn't going to hurt you or someone else? Do that. Just because you're scouring poop trails from toilets today doesn't mean you'll be scouring poop trails from toilets forever. You might. But you might not. And anyway, what a great gift to give a fellow human: a clean toilet to leave fresh poop trails in! And the fact that money comes into your life as a result of these efforts is an added delight! I dare you to try not living in the moment when you're the person who has to clean up after someone dropping a deuce and forgetting to flush it for a few days!

In addition to this, I tried to be grateful for what I DID have: the cloak of youth, a safe place to live (for one night, at least), and enough meds again—just for one day. I got a sponsor and "worked the steps," which basically means taking stock of all the bad/good that you've done, what hasn't worked out, like for me, being dramatically fearful of trying new things, or acting like a victim, or hating rich people or really anyone with a working car.

Things got better. After a year of living in the comic's spare bedroom and paying her rent in installments of a hundred dollars, I got a one-day job at an animation studio: Nicktoons (later Nickelodeon) in Studio City. Another piece of advice DA people gave was to describe my perfect "B" job. A B job, which is also a name for oral sex, is a job you're willing to do for income—and also community and improved mental health and medical benefits—while taking small steps toward your "A" job, which in LA is usually screenwriter-actor-star-epicenter-global-holdings-czar-mother-of-ten.

An animation studio fit my B job description: a creative-friendly environment (though I was a secretary) with lots of painters and animators working in the building. Also close to home, filled with plants, and sort of "fun." Now I know the realities behind cartoons—that sometimes there are hundreds of people drawing for hours in a frigid studio in South Korea who don't get anything on the back end of millions for merch tie-ins—but at the time I found it bright and colorful. Everyone working there seemed like they had some sort of creative practice outside of work, and no one was taken aback when I told them I did comedy, because they were doing their own short films or fine art or animated features.

I got another day working there, and another, and pretty soon—and I'm not sure why except that I showed up with the help of DA pals—I was hired FULL TIME for the receptionist's job! I happily anguished over the coffee supply, tea-bag caddies, and Staples orders. Because I was working more steadily, I was able to save the money to move into my own place—an efficiency in North Hollywood, which, though it had a few water bugs and a view of a muffler shop, also had a pool. A POOL! (Filled with leaves and a dead baby possum, but a POOL!) I had gotten the place with the emotional support of people in DA who helped me to look over the numbers and determine that I could afford the place and that my new job at Nickelodeon could act as credit when my credit was not good. The landlady called my mom (my only reference besides the Glendale comic) to see if my parents would cover me if I couldn't pay for some reason. My mom repeated to the landlord, "Of course not! Yeah, no. We support Maria emotionally, but not financially!" Nice boundaries, Marilyn!

After six months, I got promoted to executive secretary for a guy who would leave me dictation tapes with Post-its labeled URGENT!, RIGHT AWAY!, and ASAP! He believed that cutting out articles from *Variety* and then organizing them in a file cabinet was a good way to stay on the cutting edge of the industry. I remember there was a "Talent" section that included articles about John Leguizamo and Matt Groening, who were already extremely successful at that time. It gave me insight that maybe the people in charge knew as much as I did (which was nothing).

As seen in prior chapters, I have a beastly habit with regard to anything I am a part of: family, friendships, spiritual movements, work, open mics, life. As soon as I am embraced by something, my mind begins digging around for the negative side of it, lashing out at the gift I've been given and demonizing its existence. The perfect example: my mother.

As a kid, I felt leveled by my mom's opinion. She would scan my body up and down and say, "Huh." Then a heavy sigh. In response, I learned to imitate her voice and began repeating, onstage, some of the things she had said that bothered me the most. My mom had such a strong personality that it never occurred to me that these impersonations might hurt her feelings. I know this sounds like the oft-heard Internet-troll response, "Whoa! I didn't think you'd read your own Twitter feed!" And my mom was okay with most of it. But I'd always be surprised when she said, "Please don't say that about my Eileen Fisher clothes." (They are often black and are cut raggedly, as if for a casual civil war, torn linen pockets filled with ammunition.)

And yet I continued to do a caricatured impersonation of her to thousands of people. When I love something or someone, or am recognized as fulfilling a role (comedian, friend, neighbor, etc.), I then question its worth and give those who care about me seven heads with fangs.

My sister is a powerhouse, a superstar. In our hometown, while having coffee with a friend, I mentioned the title of one of her books, and three people around us instantly raved about it:

WHITE LADY: *Book of Beasties*! I just read that.

WHITE DUDE ON A BIKE: I'm a Dragonfly.

OTHER WHITE LADY [it's northern Minnesota]: My wife knows her!

My sister has fed me hundreds of wonderful homemade meals and once let me eat directly from her family's half gallon of organic ice cream with my bare hands as her children watched, aghast. She pointed out several years ago, in regard to my stand-up in general, "Every story you tell, you're the victim." Yes, Sarah! It's an easy arc! Victim fights for justice ending in conquest! When I was a child, there was some truth to this way of presenting things: I was pelted with pine cones on the way to school by Mike Tochter and his cronies. But now? I am no dupe. I have 92K followers on Instagram.

Given my tendency to reject those who accept me, this is the work pattern that I fight against to this day:

1. I cry in the bathroom at the impossibility or first sign that I am not good at my job (for example, upon hearing, "Did you forget to order creamer?" [receptionist], or, "Can you pace it up?" [voice-over gig]).
2. I start to see the flawed nature of my employers and the unethical moral quandaries of the job. There's a reason the animation is done in Korea! The labor is cheaper and not well-treated! There is hypocrisy in what I thought was beautiful! Now that I'm a part of it, it is BAD!
3. I start to "speak up" passive-aggressively (via comedy). At Nickelodeon, I made a satirical short film with myself and another production assistant killing off all of the Nickelodeon executives in a *Masterpiece Theatre*–style mystery.
4. I am well-liked but troubling to the people who have hired me. I do a good job, but those in charge sense my lack of respect. As with everything, once I am invited to be a part of it, it is BAD.

I was at Nickelodeon for one year and I was voted Employee of the Month the same month I got fired. After being fired, I won a voice-over role on their new series, *CatDog*. They gave me a severance of two months' pay and with that, I was able to move to a nicer neighborhood, get a dog, and begin earning more from stand-up than from temping. But I would still do anything for cash. I've answered phones for comedy development executives right after having pitch meetings with them. I worked eight hours at NBC4 reception after doing *The Tonight Show* the night before. The weatherman walked by and said, "You were on *Leno* last night!" and kept walking. The gradual change into being a full-time performer took about as long as it took me to pay off my medical debt—eight years.

WHAT IT'S LIKE NOW

Twenty-five years later, I still have a DA sponsor, I sponsor three people who call me regularly, I give PRGs once every few months, and I'll take calls from anyone in DA. It helps me get out of my own head. If you are reading this book and I haven't called you back, I'm sorry. I'm still a pig-hog sans ruffled dress. I go to meetings every week. I love an open-mic format! Just like a comedy open mic but with an ongoing reality-show story line that unspools over time, beginning with a person's initial "bottom" and gradually leading to the realization that there might be better life choices other than killing yourself. And as I've mentioned, twelve-steppers make for an easy, warm crowd.

I still go to meetings because I still need the help. And I never want to do the job I'm hired for. That includes being a TV star and writing this book, by the way. I love the initial news that I got the job, and I love the paycheck and the benefits, and I love being done. But to this day, getting to a job and staying at the job is distressing to me. I STILL SOMETIMES SLEEP IN MY CLOTHES AND SHOES SO THAT I WILL WAKE UP READY FOR WORK. That way, I don't have to go through the rigamarole of grooming that can sometimes prevent me from showing up to activities such as stand-up, relationships, and that thing that was on my vision board.

HALF-ASSED MAKES CASH. POOP IT OUT. JES DOO EEET. Read Jack Kerouac—I AM NOT LAZY *ENOUGH* TO WRITE A BOOK. And here's a new affirmation given to me by my sister, the life coach: "They hired YOU. How is it YOUR fault?" The main feeling I have after finishing a job, whether it's mopping an industrial kitchen floor or doing fifty minutes of stand-up in a black-box theater, is relief. I'm proud, but I'm also *really* glad it's over.

Another cult ideal I am a fan of is Debtors Anonymous's OPEN-BOOK ACCOUNTING. THIS IS NOT FILLER. THIS IS INFORMATION I MUST LET YOU KNOW. Do not kid yourself. I have to tell you the numbers. The benefits of transparency are several:

1. Street cred.
2. It scratches that OCD itch if you happen to suffer from an obsession with ethics.

AND MOST IMPORTANTLY

3. What if it's helpful? To you or to me to talk more openly about money so that it isn't such a shady topic of debilitating confusion and unfairness. Maybe not, but here's hoping, and most likely not.

According to Simon & Schuster, I cannot cross corporate boundaries I've agreed to. But if you meet me in person, I will tell you everything and show you my QuickBooks files. But let's just say S&S gave me twenty-five dollars to begin this work. And promised me another twenty-five dollars upon delivering a finished book. That first twenty-five dollars, however, is not really mine. As I had never written a book before, I gave that twenty-five dollars to an editor who helped me get the book written.

Now here's where it gets interesting. If they (Simon & Schuster) reject my book or if I don't finish the book, I must give all twenty-five bucks back to Simon & Schuster. This was a surprise to me, as I had read, but in no way understood, the contract. What that means is that if I don't complete this book to S&S's satisfaction, I will owe S&S twenty-five dollars for the pleasure of writing this book.

"Wait—wha?? Are you saying when you write a book, it's like incurring a debt? And that if you get paid, by the time you get paid, two and a half years will have passed, but at the rate you're going, probably four? Maria, are you still fucking up with money?"

YES! I AM A GOON. I SCREWED UP! AND OF COURSE they don't give twenty-five dollars to somebody who's never done the job and assume they'll do it! Or squeeze out a dime until they've accepted the final work! Read every biography of every writer! If this thing isn't published, I will be paying back twenty-five dollars, slowly, over time with a reasonable payment plan, for an extravagant wake-up call. The twenty-five-dollar lesson that I would learn—which holds true now and forever—is that despite telling everyone I wanted to write a book, I really didn't *want* to write a book AT ALL.

In addition to revealing the financial details of my book deal, I also wanted to include a profit-and-loss statement regarding my business. I argued with my editor AND my manager about this. MANY TIMES. PERSONALLY, *I LOVE THIS KIND OF INFO, BUT NO ONE ELSE IS INTERESTED, ESPECIALLY THE EDITORS.* If you don't care, as you were. AS YOU WERE.

GIVE CAM

Bamfooco, Inc., which consists of me and Scott, gives 11 percent of our net income to charity. That is exactly 1 (one) percent more than the Christians. Tell someone who attends a church about our generosity.

As of September 22, 2022, Bamfooco, Inc. so far has donated $27,119 to charity, which is 11 percent of . . . ? You do the math! It's fun!

Example of what I earn as a comedian as of this moment in time: it varies! This is an example of one month of shows, but it also depends on whether I am still "drawing," or my popularity as a comedian. There is no union rate for stand-up, and so contracts differ widely from artist to artist, and I am in charge of what the opener gets paid. Many times, the opener will be told that it's a valuable opportunity to open and that it pays only a hundred dollars or less, when the headliner is receiving many times more. I pay openers at least $1,200 (unless it's more than what I'm earning!). For a while, I was doing profit-sharing and hope to resume when I have a prudent reserve for the business.

PING PONG, AK	2 SHOWS	
Received	$ 7,000.00	
EXPENSES		
Airfare	$465.20	
Hotel	$663.60	
Lyft	$400.00	
Tips	$40.00	
Opening act	$1,200.00	
TOTAL	**$2,768.80**	
Commissionable	**$4,231.20**	
Gersh	$423.12	(Agent 10%)
Omnipop	$317.34	(Mgr 7.5%)
NET BAMFOOCO, INC.	$3,490.74	(Remember to take 30 percent out after this number for taxes.)
JAI-HO, BELARUS	6 shows	
Received	$17,700.00	
EXPENSES		
Airfare	$657.20	

Hotel	N/A	
Lyft	$200.00	
Tips	N/A	
Opening act	$1,200.00	
TOTAL	**$2,057.20**	
Commissionable	**$15,642.80**	
Gersh	$1,564.28	
Omnipop	$1,173.21	
NET BAMFOOCO, INC.	$12,905.79	(Again, 30 percent out for taxes! I have forgotten before! WHOOPSIE!)

A SAMPLE MONTH FOR BAMFOOCO, INC.

BAMFOOCO, INC.	
PROFIT AND LOSS	
SEPTEMBER 1–25, 2022	
	Total
INCOME	
Live shows	40,418.75
Merch	97.96
Voice-over	13,177.51
Total income	**$53,694.22**
Gross profit	**$53,694.22**
EXPENSES	
Automobile Expenses:	
Fuel	73.37
Total automobile expenses	**$73.37**
Bank service charges	54.65
Business gifts	53.18
Charitable contributions	100.00
Commissions	7,567.64

Total commissions	**$7,567.64**
Computer and internet expenses	191.99
Software	57.95
Total computer and internet expenses	**$249.94**
Continuing education	27.51
Dues and subscriptions	23.99
Editor	250.00
Employee	1,095.83
Insurance expenses:	
Life insurance	1,129.00
Total insurance expenses	**$1,129.00**
Meals and entertainment	660.04
Entertainment research:	
Books	231.87
Movies	15.49
Total entertainment research	**$247.36**
Meals 100%	860.96
Total meals and entertainment	**$1,768.36**
Payroll:	
Employee salary	10,000.00
Payroll fees	65.27
Payroll taxes	8,388.90
Total payroll	**$18,454.17**
Political contribution	250.00
Postage and delivery	33.02
Production and supplies costs	6,925.00
Merch	1,574.70
Total production and supplies costs	**$8,499.70**
Professional fees	8.00
Publicity	1,000.00
Jess Knox Guinivan	1,650.00
Total publicity	**$2,650.00**

Subcontracted services:	
Acting coach:	
Ivana Shein	400.00
Total acting coach	**$400.00**
Assistant	310.00
Melinda Hill	125.00
Total assistant	**$435.00**
Coaching:	
Melinda Hill	250.00
Total coaching	**$250.00**
Opening act	5,150.00
Jackie Kashian, Inc.	655.00
Total opening act	**$5,805.00**
Total subcontracted services	**$6,890.00**
Taxes:	
CA Franchise Tax Board	4,995.00
Total taxes	**$4,995.00**
Telephone expenses	259.68
Travel expenses	-2,500.00
Airfare	614.40
Hotels	1,248.90
Internet	49.95
Lyft	781.00
Taxi	15.94
Travel insurance	200.78
Travel meals	30.64
Total travel expenses	**$441.61**
Uncategorized expenses	-446.59
Total expenses	**$54,428.06**
Net operating income	**-$733.84**
Net income	**-$733.84**
	Sunday, Sep 25, 2022 11:44:19 AM GMT-7 - Cash Basis

I've highlighted all the numbers I fear are "shameful" in some way. (For example, that I'm not giving enough to charity: I do the 11 percent calculation on exactly how much I receive out of the business—so my salary plus any draw I take—but it isn't perfect, and I'm always worried it's incorrect.) LET ME KNOW if you don't think it's enough, feel angry that I am doing it improperly, are generally disappointed in me, or think that I should be ashamed of myself and why at ariamaamfordba@gmail.com or at the very least "@" me on social media with a diss. Tag me with something damningly astute that I will repost before I try to make friends with you in your DMs, asking you what YOU think I should do with the money. And then, when you refuse, I will mute you so I don't have to be reminded of our falling-out. You are right, internet, you are always right. It would be an honor to learn something and I am being sincere. I LOVE YOU SO MUCH.

RECIPE FOR BOOKKEEPING WHILE EATING PEANUT BUTTER BETWEEN PIECES OF CHEESE

1. Let peanut butter and cheese residue build up on your keyboard over a period of three years while writing this book.
2. Don't worry about it.

12. OCD CBT THAT IS NOT FREE

Biting the Hand That Feeds can be profitable and therefore healing. Being a judgmental Judy about every experience I have and person I meet pays our property taxes. Impersonating family members was part of the stand-up material that allowed me to transition from office work to comedy. Impersonating people at my office jobs led me to get more stand-up jobs, which paid more than full-time office work and entitled me to have the wherewithal to google "unwanted thoughts" and blow three hundred bones on an OCD specialist in Glendale who doesn't take insurance. With more cash, I had the time and energy to get real help and then follow through on the therapeutic interventions assigned to me. I had the time to google "not wanted," "violent thoughts," "sexual thoughts," "unwanted," plus my zip code (90004), and up came RODNEY BOONE, MD, PhD, of Glendale and the Cognitive Behavioral Therapy Center of Southern California, a mere three miles from me. I made an appointment!

Dr. $300 an Hour is a man who helped me tremendously, and his hand remains unbitten. I think he still practices but is pricey. (I recommend www.treatmyocd.com and the www.iocdf.org for lower- to no-cost internet access to OCD treatment. I have since used both these organizations and have done paid advertising for them: full disclosure.) At the first appointment, through closed eyes, I told him vaguely about my lifelong fear that I was a serial-raper-murder-molester-genocider (despite the lack of desire, plan, or evidence of such behavior). He looked appropriately, professionally interested, but also GLORIOUSLY BORED. He had heard it all before. We started CBT, cognitive behavioral therapy, the "gold standard" for OCD treatment.

Firstly, Dr. Boone told me to write down my worst fears, describing them in as much detail as I could bear. He said to write these things as if they were happening RIGHT NOW, in the present tense, all the way to the final result. For example: "I am now cutting off the ears of my father and despite his screams, I begin scissoring off his nose," all the way to the imagined end result: "With my father's decoupaged corpse, the cops surround me, and I am put in the general population of a central California prison and no one is taking my calls." Well, that sounded sort of possible—though very dangerous and irresponsible. Like, who writes stuff like that down? A SERIAL-RAPER-MURDERER-MOLESTER-GENOCIDER, THAT'S WHO. But I did it. It was extremely scary but also a very confusing relief to write it ALL DOWN and realize that there was sort of an anticlimactic end point—one that was kind of funny—after my worst fears of myself came true: once I was locked away in solitary confinement and after sentencing by the judge . . . I'd just be ALONE. There was nothing more to do after I had gone through all of the horrible things.

I brought back this exciting essay to Dr. Boone and he said, "Great, now record what you've written and for one hour a day listen to it over and over again." I tried to tell him that it sounded illegal, but he assured me that I'd be the only person ever to hear it. It's part of a process called "flooding," where you get so used to being in a high state of anxiety that your brain gets accustomed to the thoughts so it no longer gets anxious, finding previously terrifying thoughts tedious. The only thing the doctor said I couldn't do was try to get away from the thoughts or turn off the recording before one hour was up, or in any other way avoid the feelings of panic. I was just to sit and ride it out and notice that the panic eventually peaked and went down. With his support, I did it the whole next week.

I came back and he said, "Okay, now do something you avoid doing because of the thoughts." The one thing I'd never do is spend much alone time with a friend. I could do maybe thirty minutes tops, and then I'd get too anxious and have to leave. He said, "Go to a friend's house where you're alone together and stay for two hours and tell me how it goes." This part felt *terrible.* Spending time alone with a friend was a major trigger for The Fears.

I made a date to hang out with my pal Solange. I listened to my horrifying monologue of sexual violence on the forty-five-minute drive over. I called Dr. Boone. I went in. Solange and I hung out for two hours. (Solange was not aware of the therapeutic value of our hang—though she is now if she reads this!) And off and on during that time I felt really bad but had a few moments where I totally forgot about my Fears, which was a brand-new experience. Then I left and called Dr. Boone to say how it went. (No one was hurt!)

Since that night, with a few surges of OCD of different types over the years—I get new fears now—I have been mostly free and clear of mindfucks that had weighed on me my whole life. Thanks, Dr. Boone. Thank you, internet. And thank you to me and my unattractive habit of criticizing everything that has ever shown me love.

COFFEE FOR TWO

1. Get one of those "concentrated" jugs of cold brew coffee.
2. Pour a "shot" of concentrated cold brew. It's just coffee.
3. Drink it like a tequila shot.
4. Go to the gym.
5. Get on a StairMaster.
6. Unable to stand, legs wobbling, fall off the machine.
7. From the gym floor, text your spouse for help.
8. Make your way outside, crawling, holding on to the wall.
9. Your spouse arrives, looking amused.
10. Your loved one shakes their head, helping you into the car, calling you a monkey.

13. My ?th (Who Cares) Cult: Sex and Love Addicts Anonymous

(I love to label and pathologize human instincts!)

MONEY RAISED IN TWELVE-STEP PROGRAMS IS NOT GOING INTO LOGO DESIGN.

Due to my fear of human contact—as well as to my occasional (yearly) need for it—in my twenties and early thirties I was a big fan of the one-night stand. Because of the romance-novel standards of my First Love high school boyfriend, I couldn't seem to connect with anyone. It was after a one-night stand with a writer in Texas—who may actually not have been a writer but just a guy who had books—that I started to worry.

It can be pretty gross, the one-night stand. This one was at an Econo Lodge. I hadn't ever had someone do "dirty talk" with me. This gent did that without any warning or warm-up and it was El Súper Extranjero. "Slut" wasn't the empowering adjective it is today. I was totally turned off and wanted him to leave, but I couldn't get myself to say anything. I had trouble stopping a one-night stand once it was put in motion. I didn't want to have relations with this book-owning person, but I did anyway and it felt like I couldn't stop myself.

What to do? I joined another twelve-step group! Sex and Love Addicts Anonymous. WHAT? THAT'S A THING? YES AND IT'S FREE!

As you can imagine, the type of addiction colors the vibe of the group. AA is rowdy, like a party or a bar—lots of joshing and camaraderie. Overeaters Anonymous is mostly quiet types who would rather be alone with a turtle sundae or a roasted chicken. Al-Anon (for family and friends of addicts) is high-strung; there are tons of formatted readings and mutually managed control freaks. Debtors Anonymous has a business seminar feel, and they use parliamentary procedure to decide what kind of bagels to serve at the meeting.

An SLAA meeting looks something like when the lights come on at the end of the night at the club. It is filled with buzzy, intense people in tight clothes. These are people who could seduce an entire room with their bracing eye colors. And on the other hand, there are more introverted types who, before recovery, might have let their hands slip while giving you an unwanted backrub. It was a real shock to hear a hawt dude—someone whom I'd identify as "hawt" before "human"—cry and say he wanted to stop sleeping with strangers. It had never occurred to me that dudes or hawt people in general didn't want to have one-night stands or obsessive types of relationships anymore either. I'd experienced meaningful change with the other twelve-steps, so I went for it, got a sponsor who was a former sex worker and now a sex therapist, "worked the steps," the whole shebang.

And woo-hoo, with SLAA I stopped having sex with total strangers!

Which isn't a bad thing unless it's a bad thing for YOU! I was able to stop with the information that:

- in having one-night stands, I might be victimizing or manipulating someone else—and that it's not just "for fun" unless there's some discussion and understanding up front and even that discussion will create intimacy (which I'm afraid of!).
- it's important to define what a relationship isn't—that I shouldn't expect any more from a romantic partner than I should from a friend. The same number of issues and disappointments that I have with my ratchet friends (that includes me) should also be in my intimate partnerships if we're both human beings.

And I got a dating plan! This isn't a mandated thing. SLAA, like OA, has sort of a "you do you" sobriety model. But a dating plan was a format to slow down the process of getting to know someone. Of course, as soon as I started dating, I got into a relationship right away. With a clown in New Zealand. (Hold for laughs.)

It was an improvement. It was much better than I HAD been doing.

I had met a red-rubber-nosed New Zealander—a fellow artist—at a comedy festival. He was very funny, super cute, single, and seemed into me! This doesn't happen to me in real-world scenarios. HOW PERFECT! And then all of the signs of it probably not being a great idea were there:

- He lived in New Zealand.
- He brought a date to our second date. (She was very nice. He explained that he couldn't cancel on her after asking me out too? Oh. Wait. What?)
- There was a bananas sense of attraction (hypomania on my part).

- He didn't like "fame" and looked down on any glossy signs of success (my poster was all over the city).
- He had a nude one-man show that he toured worldwide about a young man coming into his (gay) sexuality.

However, it was an excellent set of training wheels for having my first semi-real relationship since the age of nineteen. We had a whirlwind of six dates (the number mandated by my SLAA dating plan). I asked him (via SLAA guidelines) if we were in a committed relationship, so that we could have sex. He was down, we got down, and we made plans that I'd come visit him in NEW ZEALAND (where he lived as a mostly unemployed itinerant minstrel), which would amazingly be made possible by the NZ government. Flight of the Conchords, I'm in!

I went home and began planning. I was so relieved to be leaving LA! The United States didn't "get" my sense of humor anyway! If I still believed in God, this was definitely some sort of Holy Sure Thing. I am meant to be a New Zealander. I researched how to relocate to NZ, read expatriate memoirs of people who moved to NZ, memorized ALL FIVE VERSES of the NZ national anthem (which no New Zealanders know). I made lists of things I would need to do in order to move: sell furniture, complete my dog's paperwork to emigrate, find all the twelve-step groups in NZ. I was READY. I flew over to visit him. I got off the flight in Auckland. This was before cell phones. And NZ clown man wasn't there. HE FORGOT TO PICK ME UP at the airport.

Did I mention he lived in a condo RIGHT outside the airport—like a thousand yards away, right beneath the flight path? I exchanged some money and got on a pay phone to call him. He picked up and said, "Oh, yes! Right-o!" and he came over the quarter mile so I wouldn't have to pay for a cab. Not a great sign. He forgot to pick up this person he said he was crazy about, after I'd flown eighteen hours to see him. But Maria, you know the national anthem—it's got to work! Do not dwell on this detail! I'm in recovery from romantic anorexia (a real term)!

Now here's where I got, as the '90s male comics would say, "psycho" (which is not a diagnosis). I had told him I was just coming for two weeks, when I had actually planned to visit for three months. Upon arriving at his apartment, I informed him about my plans of staying for three months. At his place. With his unenthusiastic permission, I did. It was not good. He was pissed, but in his excitingly desirable wishy-washy style, he acquiesced.

We were perfect for each other. I was terrified of commitment to any person, and he was decisive in his muddy feelings about me.

NZ CLOWN: I love you, but I cannot have sex with you. I'm overwhelmed by your body.

No worries, as the Ozzies next door say! I lived in NZ for a year with him. Twelve months in, I gratefully read a new book from the US called *He's Just Not That Into You* and broke up with him, flying home the next day. But TWELVE MONTHS! AN SLAA WIN!

He is now married to a man with three boys! Mazel tov!

Next was Peter. He was a principal at a private school. We did six dates in six weeks. He had a lot of black-tie fundraisers to go to. I didn't have a lot of fancy clothes, nor is my wardrobe my hobby, so I borrowed something for the first event we went to, and he said, upon seeing me in it: "Oof." And FYI, I looked SLAMMING. After his negging, I got a bit sad-face in the car with wet cheeks, which is my Minnesota gal way of saying FUCK YOU. He was ticked off that I was so sensitive. Well, maybe don't thumbs-down my Project Runway as I climb into a limo in wobbly high heels?

Peter's best friend was a hard-core, not-even-trying-to-hide-it bulimic. He was a fitness junkie/fashionisto. The guy binged and headed straight to the bathroom right in front of us. None of us ever mentioned it as it was happening. Like, "Text us if you're bleeding out in the toilets!" It was unsettling. Similar to his best friend, Peter had lived a "hidden life" for two years. This hidden life was now somehow over? It involved high-risk behaviors like meth and unprotected gay sex. And again, that's ALL GOOD, but I'm the FIRST person you've told? You might want to run that by a therapist before you spill it to the lady you've been dating for a few weeks (says the bipolar comic who tells hundreds of strangers everything, read from a notebook soaked with warm Diet Coke drippings).

The final straw came at six weeks, when I had been talking about something I was excited about (probably twelve-step programs), and he seemed visibly clocked out, looking around and then down to his phone. I know now that a little tedium is the basis of intimacy in most relationships—there is an obligation in love to listen to your best friend's new obsession with miniature Doberman pinscher athletic trials, your mom's encyclopedic knowledge of P. D. James mysteries, or, in this case, your very hot girlfriend's constant reflections and revelations about a group you are not a part of. Suck it up! You are trying to LOVE someone! LISTEN TO THE EMOTION BEHIND THE WORDS!

Anyhoo, that last disconnect, combined with the fact that I disliked his feature-length horror film, made it easier to text a break-up after six weeks. Text a break-up? That is cold. Yes. I am a not-good fuckchop.

Next up: Andy. Again, I moved a little too fast. We did six dates over six weeks, as recommended by my SLAA sponsor, but it was a pretty crazy feeling. I had a hard time thinking about anyone else. Andy was a writer, in Marijuana Anonymous, and very volatile/charming. (Me too!) I was a hyper-sad sack and therefore a great match. Andy's a hilarious person and there were some good laughs, but he'd get paranoid that I was flirting with other people at MA meetings (I wasn't and am not sure what that would possibly look like), and once he said (out loud, while staring into my eyes) in a romantic setting, "I would never hit you." We visited my family together in Duluth, and my mom and sister sat me down privately to express concern that I might be in danger, as Andy seemed "scary." They didn't say what I seemed like.

Andy and I made it eleven months!

RECIPE FOR A TWELVE-STEP DATE

One of the best memories I have of Andy is of handing him this sandwich:

- 2 heels of bread
- 3-inch-thick layer of peanut butter, spread evenly, like frosting, to edge of each heel
- 2 tablespoons jelly in the middle

1. Squish sandwich so that the jelly might reach edges of heel.
2. Overwrap in tinfoil, two or three layers, like a bomb.
3. Hand to your boyfriend in the middle of a twelve-step meeting as "dinner."
4. Watch him try to eat it.
5. Bring him a Styrofoam cup of coffee, as he choke-laughs down every bite.

14. The Cult of Success

EVERYTHING WAS GOING REALLY GREAT!

By 2008, I'd been in LA for a little over a decade, and after more than ten years of auditioning, I was NOT getting any acting jobs unless I was in a bad mood (a California Lottery ad chose me for my hilarious character "take" of "pissed that the auditions were going so long, because I had to get back to work"). I told my manager, Bruce, that in terms of cost-benefit analysis—ten years of auditioning for acting roles vs. three thousand dollars in earnings total—it was better to focus everything on stand-up, which, at the time, earned me around $75K per year, regularly, and it was fun. Bruce was suggested to me by my old manager, who got out of the managing business probably due to the ongoing difficulty of dealing with low-earning nincompoops like myself. I am forever grateful.

At one point (in the Lake Superior pond of Duluth, where only five people total auditioned for the entire cast of *Les Misérables*), I LOVED AUDITIONING. I HATED auditioning in LA. I didn't understand how people "booked." In LA, I felt like the water was teeming with so many beautiful fish and I realized it'd be better to beach myself. And so I entered the World of Offer-Only.

I cannot recommend offer-only enough. You know that thing you never get to do because it's too competitive and it's too painful to even try for fun because you've spent over ten thousand hours getting paid at the most .07 cents per hour to do it? Are you tired of doing free work for possible prestige? Possible opportunities on spec, but no financial reward? "Offer-only" means that you will only agree to do that kind of job again if there is a contract in place paying you union rate with an additional promise that if you get fired, you will get paid for your time. For example:

SHOWBIX: Hey, ACTOR! We'd really like to see you memorize five dramatic scenes for a film project and you'll have to drive to Venice at rush hour to perform it for what seems like an abused spouse/production assistant?

ME: Oh, no thanks. I'd love to, but I'm "offer-only." I will do any job to earn money instead of auditioning. That includes working at a dry-cleaning plant and yes, I have experience working at a dry-cleaning plant.

SHOWBIX: Well, too bad, this could have been your chance.

ME: I know.

SHOW BISCUIT: Hey, SUPERSTAR! We would love to see you at 9 p.m. on a Tuesday in downtown LA to "read" for something?

ME: Oh, yeah, no, I have friends and we do things together like eat. I'm "offer-only."

I can't wait to see the movie *BLOCKBUSTER* in the theater.

SHOW BISCUIT: You could have read for an INTERNATIONAL MEGAHIT! You are AN ABSOLUTE MORON!

ME: I know.

SHOWBIDNAZ: Hey, BEAUTIFUL! FANCY DANCY has a live theater show and they LOVE-SNUG-HUMP you. Can you PLEASE drive three hours round trip for forty dollars to do ten minutes of stand-up to an audience that is really there to see THE HUMAN EMPIRE STATE BUILDING?

ME: Oh, I'm sorry. I'm booked to stare at the moon.

SHOWBIDNAZ: But they CRAVE you and they are IMPORTANT and you ADMIRE THEM!!! Won't you just make a little effort, just a five-hour window, to connect with the REAL DEAL, the cream of the cropped pants?

ME: No. But I will watch their award-winning films with JOY AND APPRECIATION. I would prefer doing an hour-long show to someone across a table from me in the back of my favorite coffee shop less than a mile from my house. There is an internet record of them being a fan, I'm done with work at noon, and everybody gets a drink of their choosing at Café de Leche Altadena.

In 2008, I got featured in an ad campaign (without auditioning, just an offer of $) for a company I buy from regularly whose product line is also linked to positive memories from childhood. This vendor is known as the TARGET Corporation. I may have begun feeling a little "off" at this time . . . believing in God, in "signs," in "the plan." Advertising for Target surely must be a part of God's Plan. The advertising campaign was creatively developed in PORTLAND, Oregon. Portland is GOOD! PORTLAND PLUS TARGET EQUALS DOUBLE-GOOD GOD, GOD GOOD!!

I love and have always loved Target. My friend's dad died recently, and the family was sitting around after the funeral, depressed. Somebody suggested, "Does anyone want to go to Target?" Everybody did. They did a post-wake Target run, and she said it cheered everybody up. Of course it did. Target is a brightly colored promise of tomorrow!

The Christmas campaign I was in seemed to be a success (in my eyes). "People" LOVE IT, love the character. The character is compulsively shopping by herself in a hilariously sad way, a harebrained retail addict who dressed beautifully in red and white. It's a great character for progressives who shop at Target, because it's darkly funny in a Portland-y kind of way. Like, "WE GET IT," and you also get to overbuy cheaply made items from across the globe—items that you don't want to think about where they came from, just like the conservatives. Just because you're right about everything doesn't mean you can't waste your money on crap and have a little consumer FUN!

For me, it feels great financially, creatively, to do this job. But I'm starting to feel more and more sort of "out of control" with the increased responsibility and "success," as once there is success, there is just more to do. And slowly, I realize—and I knew this from the contract, but I didn't know how it would feel—that I can't talk about Target publicly in any way. When the ad comes out, I am announced by a comic emcee as a "sellout"—a joke, but sometimes jokes are just a statement of fact. I feel uncomfortable. To feel better about myself, I repost a critique of working conditions in overseas manufacturing of clothing (not mentioning Target). I am asked within two hours by the advertising agency in Portland to take down the post.

Oh!! Wow! Okay!

The next Christmas, 2009, is even more fun! Because people have liked the previous campaign! My pay goes up! And the only issue is that the more people are exposed to the commercials, the more it's starting to affect my stand-up shows. People start coming to shows expecting the Target lady and are surprised to hear my elaborate word salads about depression. The Target job is effectively ruining stand-up, as I'm starting to get crowds who don't know what they've come to see.

I'm also starting to meet Target employees. They tell me how they believe Target is a union-buster, they're barely making ends meet, and that Target is no better than Walmart when it comes to benefits. WOOOF. Uh-oh. I am a union member. Over social media, fans forward me a union-busting in-house Target video starring my fellow SAG union members "acting" as Target team members, telling these underpaid people that they shouldn't organize. The reason I am treated so well, have health care, and have a roof over my head is directly because I am IN A UNION. Whoops.

As part of an internet content loophole, I get a taste of being non-union when I'm hired by Target to do some commercials for the web. It is 115 degrees inside of an unfinished new house (owned by the producer) with no plumbing or AC in Bel Air. In the blistering heat, I am put in a snowsuit and tasked with joyful, over-the-top act-outs while dancing. I am dying. I have low blood pressure: I run cold, but even I am overheating. It's five hours in, but there are enough bottles of lukewarm water on set. I can do it. We get a half-hour break for lunch. There is nowhere to go. I pass out on a pile of plywood that is the temp of the surface of the sun. HEY NOW! Wake up! It's back to work. I put on my snowsuit again and down my eighth bottle of water. Did I mention the directors were from Austria and that their primary requests were that I be "FUNNIER, FASTER"? We get to hour twelve. I cannot focus. I am struggling in a way I don't recognize. They are asking me to spin in an office chair while saying lines like, "The Target Black Friday sale starts NOW, sugarplums!" It is at that point that I—involuntarily—begin to heave-cry. Dressed in a Target-red Prada tailored wool business suit, I detach the mic; yawp "I'm sorry" while hyperventilating; and walk off set in four-inch heels.

The way out of the construction site is a deeply rutted mud road uphill. I stumble to my car despite PAs yelling, "Are you okay?" Uh, no, not okay. I drive away, calling my DA sponsor at the time, Noel, and he says, "BREATHE and call your manager." I call Bruce and tell him, through tears, "I [*snort*] need [*sucking air*] a [*wheeze*] moment." I come back the next day and shoot the rest of the scenes.

I began to wonder, "Is this Target thing really a 'God shot'? Does God know that Target might outsource its production of goods to countries where there are few to no environmental protections or labor laws to make sure its bright, FUN FASHIONS and HOMEWARES are so cheap? Does God know that Target might limit the hours of employees to part time so that they don't have to give health benefits and pay a living wage, so that their employees have to use the charities and food banks that Target gets tax breaks to donate to? God? Hey, God. TMB. God, are you trying to tell me that I'm supposed to become a whistle-blowing activist for fair wages worldwide? I feel like that's what you're saying, I'll try to get a second opinion from my twelve-step pals who are telling me I'm talking too fast. . . ."

WEIGHT-LOSS RECIPE

1. Get a prescription for Wellbutrin.

15. I Killed God (and the Circumstances Leading Up to a Breakdown)

Susan Maljan

When I think of a God, I think of my dog, Blossom.

If you have met a pug, or any other affectionate animal, you might be able to understand its unique qualifications for being an Omnipotent Life Force.

As mentioned, my time in Debtors Anonymous had many positive outcomes, like when, after countless hours on the phone, my DA sponsor suggest-commanded, "You have to move to a nicer neighborhood and get a dog!" My North Hollywood apartment's pool had filled with leaves (that I swam in anyway), and the landlord—a very sweet old man with an oversize toupee—had shot himself in the head in a room facing my bedroom, so maybe it was time for a change.

Since I was doing better professionally, I was able to save up a first- and last-month deposit, and I found a dog-friendly one-bedroom in Los Feliz, a hip, walkable, centrally located area in LA.

I took quizzes online to see what breed would be good for my personality (and vice versa). According to my need for affection and low energy level, the pug was perfect. At the time, because I hadn't ever had a dog, I was afraid to apply at the rescue organizations. I called around to breeders and found PUGGIESRUS of Costa Mesa, then I drove to a minimanse and sat in someone's living room. A dirty old pug came barreling up to me, sitting right in my lap. The guy said she was two and that he wanted three hundred dollars for her. I later brought her to the vet, who said, "She's eight years old if she's a day, and she stinks." Her name was Chula, but I named her Blossom, after *The Powerpuff Girls.*

On our first walk together in Los Feliz, her teats were distended enough that a stranger approached us and suggested a plastic surgeon. After bringing her home, hilariously, I wasn't sure if I could handle it. But a week passed, and I started doing attachment exercises (for me, not Blossom) that I had read about people doing with kids adopted from Russian orphanages. I'm not sure who the orphan was in this scenario, but the exercises included engaging in bouts of extended eye contact with Blossom—a technique called "holding"—several times a day in an effort to bond her to me and vice versa. She didn't seem to mind, and I felt very comforted by it.

We went everywhere together. We would walk a mile to the gym and because she couldn't make the walk back, I would carry her like a baby. I began traveling with her in a roller bag. Every time I left the house she barked nonstop, probably because of the attachment exercises. I put a bark-preventing orange citrus spray collar on her, but this just ended with her barking uncontrollably with her face drenched in orange juice. Then I shared about the problem at a DA meeting and a twelve-stepper came over and for forty-five dollars introduced me to an anti-barking technique that, though quirky and possibly upsetting to onlookers, did work.

Here's the training:

You say the same thing and do the same thing EVERY. TIME. YOU. LEAVE. THE. HOUSE. Cheerfully! No stress!

"I'm going. I'll be back. Watch the house!"

Then you shut the door and wait.

As soon as you hear even the slightest whimper or cry, you burst dramatically back into the apartment and scream: "NOOOOOO!"

Then you go about your business in the apartment as if you didn't just scream, "NOOOOOO!" Act super normal. Maybe fluff pillows for a minute. Then you repeat, cheerfully: "I'm going. I'll be back. Watch the house!"

And you stand silently outside the door waiting for any sound. It might take a little longer this time for your dog to start crying. Let's say it's one minute. Then burst in: "NOOOOOOOOOOOO!"

And you repeat the nonchalant act of going about your beeswax for thirty seconds or so. Then you do it all again, and each time the dog takes longer and longer to start crying until finally she doesn't cry at all and forgets that you've left. The whole training process takes about two hours. It looks and sounds bad, but it worked. (I had to do it all over again any time I left Blossom in a hotel room, which caused some concern, I'm sure, at Red Roof Inns nationwide.)

I was not a perfect parent to Blossom. When I went on the road for work, sometimes I put her in the vet kennel for fifty dollars a night and felt bad about it; she got a few walks a day, but it was no Doggy Day Care or Camp Barkaway (seventy-five dollars a night). Though I made sure she got Greenies dental chews, Blossom got dry food. I paid for her to have eight rotted teeth removed; I got her hernia fixed. I brought Blossom as a wingman to a progressive Christian church in the neighborhood in order to try to make friends and community. (I told the priest I was an atheist and just in it for the cookies and singalongs and he said, "No problem! Glad to have you!") Blossom attended despite the fact she was Roman Catholic. And we had to sit in the balcony as I guess some people in the congregation were "allergic" to "dogs." The postshow after-party was held outside in a courtyard, where we both got plenty of sugary cookie crumbs.

At one point, about five years into our relationship, I went on tour for three months and had Blossy stay with a friend from church. Blossom got so depressed that she wouldn't eat unless my friend taking care of her sat on the floor next to her and ate something too, in communion. Baby never dines alone.

Blossom's greatest gift was a radical acceptance. Even if I had scary thoughts of OCD, even if I was smelly, even if I had weird black hairs on my chin, Blossom wanted to hang out with me. It's true, she wasn't particularly interested in comedy, but she would watch me perform for a good five seconds until she drifted off to sleep. She was the epitome of a Good Girl. If I stood too long in one place at the dog park, she would pee on me, as if to say, "This is mine." I had never had anyone take that kind of proud ownership of me.

So when I think of a God, I think of her. Blossom the Awesome Pug embodied Lovingkindness. Her bulbous brown eyes never wavered. She had a real and present interest in everything that I did—just like a God is supposed to.

We slept face-to-face, her breathing my breath, me breathing hers. Best Pals Forevz.

I was a bad person. And yet, she just scooted closer and leaned in. After I bought a house I couldn't afford in 2007, we moved and added Bert, an old blind pug, to the mix. Both of them were doing fine. It was me—with two mortgages (together totaling three times what my rent had been); a successful, making-me-crazy commercial campaign; and increased international touring as a stand-up—who started to get the yips.

My brain was slipping. And one day, I let Blossom down.

Bert, the new pug, had a habit of tipping over the garbage can in our kitchen while looking for chow. This could easily have been solved once and for all (and eventually was, by Scott, when he came over to the house for the first time) by putting a brick at the bottom of the garbage can. My own temporary solution, implemented one day while Bert was outside and I had to run to a voice-over audition for an hour, was to remove the ramp leading inside the house.

The house foundation was about three feet high, and so the doggie door had a ramp attached and leading down to the backyard. When I removed the ramp, Bert would be stuck in the backyard with no way to get in or get to the garbage can (which seemed like a great idea at the time). Blossom was on the inside, sans ramp, with no way of getting out (which I know now was a deadly misstep on my part).

I should simply have picked up Bert, put the garbage can on the kitchen table, and then left. But I didn't. I kicked the ramp away from inside the house and rushed to my Very Important Voice-Over Audition. I completely forgot that Blossom was around fifteen years old and would likely wake up from her slumber in the bedroom and stumble out the dog door to the now-nonexistent ramp, thus plummeting from a three-and-a-half-foot cliff.

She died of her injuries in the hour and a half I was away. I found her stiff and lifeless body at the foot of where she fell from the doggie doorway.

Of course, it was an accident. Of course I didn't mean to kill God. But I did. And now God was not around to tell me that I was okay, because I had inadvertently killed Her.

My friend Amy, whom I called mid-wail, got a crematorium to pick her little body up and we had a service for Blossom a week later, spreading her ashes on the lawn where she liked to poop and pouring out a forty-ounce Modelo in her honor.

As anyone who experiences a tragedy (which is everyone) knows, LIFE JUST KEEPS GOING. I hadn't been feeling well anyway, I'd killed my dog by accident due to being out of my gourd with distraction, and then I just kept moving, working, and internet dating with light episodes of freaking out (shrieking into pillows and caterwauling in the shower).

About a week after All Meaning Left the World, I had to shoot another Christmas campaign for Target in Portland. In this showbiz enviro, I got treated like a superstar despite being the Worst Person of All Time. I did my best to participate in the acting job when I was not back at the hotel, yawp-sobbing into my hands. I tried to stop up the sound with a 10,000-thread-count feather pillow, but I'm sure some poor souls beneath the penthouse suite heard my howling.

16. The Breakdown Begins

I am not feeling well. I cannot stop thinking about the death of God, the mortgage, and the ethical question of whether it is okay or not for me to be a spokesperson (even as a character) for a company whose actions and products I don't fully support. This is an agitated time, so I don't remember the sequence of events, but here's a few of the things I did during the next few months:

1. I drive to Santa Barbara for a twelve-step retreat to talk to a priest to see what he thinks. This Father AA is kind of a "big deal" on the circuit. He gives me an audience for my query. In response to my need for advice he says, "Well, I just bought these pants from Target."

   I explain to him that I think the employees (domestic and international) are prevented from unionizing, and describe my concerns around gross consumerism, the pollution from shipping, the contributions to global climate change.

   ME: So, knowing that, would *you* do advertisements for Target?

   AA: Huh. I guess not. It sounds pretty bad. Maybe I should return these pants.

2. Whipped and dipped in pressured speech, I speed-speak (in the rushed soliloquy of a used-car salesman) with a professor of urban and environmental policy from Occidental College over coffee about how I can still keep the job as the character AND rise up on behalf of workers. The professor is totally into my pitch (I bought him a cappuccino) and wants to strategize, but I leave the coffee shop and never contact him again.
3. I write the *New York Times* Ethicist. This is somewhere in their archives, from 2011. I couldn't find it online. My letter is chosen and so I get to speak to the Ethicist over the phone personally. I explain to him, in rapid staccato, my endlessly fascinating (to me), life-or-death conundrum. He simply says, "Yeah. You shouldn't do it. Even if it's a character, you're advocating for the brand. You are propaganda."

The Ethicist column runs. An exec at Target (who is also a friend) calls me and asks if I wrote the letter. I lie and say it wasn't me. I have a feeling he knows it's me, and I am never asked to do Target commercials again. WOO-HOO?

I follow up my loss of employment with a Christmas party. In a crazily democratic gesture, I invite everyone I've ever emailed on my Gmail account over the course of the previous five years.

When you think about how many people you email over just one year, including customer-service representatives and other randos, the average person probably has more than five thousand people in her inbox. By clicking on a photo of dish towels, I now have fifty new friends who contact me every day to tell me about Magnolia and its subsidiaries.

The home I owned at the time was nine hundred square feet.

Here are just a few of the people who attended that Christmas party:

- A bank teller I once asked about having extra fees removed from my checking account. He brought a purple velvety bag (of Crown Royal—very classy) and four friends.
- A guy off Craigslist I had gone on one coffee date with and who was now married with a child.
- A friend from ten years ago whom I'd stopped talking to when they moved to Northern California and who had become extremely wealthy due to marriage.
- Hundreds and hundreds of strangers.

I want to say it was only 150 people who showed up that night, but I have a feeling it was more like an ongoing stream of five hundred guests. It was, like me, a bit out of control. The cops didn't come because there wasn't any bumping music, but I apologize to anyone living next to me at the time: Carlos and Diane to the left and Marta and Leo to the right.

Maria, where was your psychiatrist in all this? Well, I had been on 40 to 80 mg of Prozac since going through treatment for an eating disorder in 1990. And that's what I wanted to stay on. My psychiatrist at the time, Dr. 25 Bucks a Pop, took my insurance and was less than five miles from me: close and cheap is what I like in my health-care provider. I had been going to her since I bought the house I couldn't afford in Eagle Rock. She kept suggesting mood stabilizers. I told her I was good with just Prozac, that I needed to have energy to work, that I couldn't abide the side effects of weight gain and sleepiness. Suicidal thoughts are okay, but five pounds and ten hours of sleep a night—no thank you!

It was Dr. Woodall's theory that I might have bipolar of the II variety, due to all the spurts of energy and crying jags. There are two kinds of bipolar disorder: There's the Patty Duke bipolar I, where you have rapid cycling, psychosis, way up and way down, paranoia. And then there's bipolar II, which is some light mania, no psychosis, and mixed states of depression/obsession, plus the chutzpah to do something about it. The good doctor wanted to put me on a medicine called Depakote.

My mom was on Depakote (a mood stabilizer) in order to prevent her from having seizures. She was on this med from age twenty-five to seventy-four. When she went off it, she had a full manic episode.

Did my mom have some kind of bipolar disorder? I never thought she did until I read the symptoms of it:

- Having higher-than-normal energy levels (would really want to get things CLEAN, PERFECT, DONE! I WANT THIS HOUSE PICKED UP!!!!! [BUT THE HOUSE IS ALREADY PICKED UP?]).
- Being restless or unable to sit still (my mom knitted without ceasing).
- Having a decreased need for sleep (not sure about this, but my mom was PUMPED!).
- Having increased self-esteem or confidence or grandiosity. (This only happened a few times, but when it did happen, my mom would cackle angrily about Penny Goshawker and how "Penny Goshawker is no Mary Thorpe! I'll tell you that much!")
- Being extremely talkative.
- Having a *racing mind*, or having lots of new ideas and plans (REDECORATING! SHOPPING, TRAVEL!).
- Having decreased inhibitions. (No. My mom was fairly shy except during one full manic episode when she yelled at people in the hospital and told everyone my sister was the devil. And that I was an angel. Ha-ha! She finally got it right.)

- Having increased sexual desire. (Yikes. I will just say my mom was verbally confident in having a healthy sex life. It was important to her that we knew she was getting some. I am not sure why my parents boned every day, as it should be?)

My mom claimed that the reason she took Depakote was because of seizures that she had in her twenties. Yet she was still on Depakote forty years later, and when she tried to go off it in her seventies along with adding an injection of a steroid for a physical ailment, she went full manic and tried to leave her marriage of fifty years and drive to the Twin Cities with ten thousand dollars in cash. (She was hospitalized involuntarily and put back on Depakote.) I did talk about this episode with my mother several times, but she distanced herself from the idea that it was at all related to any bipolar tendencies.

I did not want to go on Depakote. I told Dr. Woodall I would think about going on a new medication called Lamictal but that I could only take a weekend off work for the transition.

Anyway, the wildest thing about the party is that at the time *I* didn't think it was wild. Oh, it's Lloyd, my mailman! I forgot I asked him too! He's still wearing his uniform and drinking straight from a bottle of wine! And here is every young comedian I've ever met (the more seasoned comedians stayed away from my enormous Evite) and every local business I've ever had contact with! Open bar is on the gentrifier!

Suffice it to say, everything was "perfect." I was doing well with my career (except for the Target thing and God, aka Blossom)! I was 125 pounds! I was doing stand-up internationally! I had BOUGHT A HOUSE IN LOS ANGELES COUNTY! I just had a massive party! My doctor says I should try a mood stabilizer, okay! I'll try it in my new house I just bought! But then my dog died! And it was my fault! I'm great! I have tons of work! I don't feel good! And the doctor keeps saying I'm a little herky-jerky-turkey! Then there it was: I met *The Perfect Person*. The person I was meant to meet because I deserved it! That'll sort it!

He was a great professional writer, and he was from Canada! He was divorced, so presumably understood pain, and he was VERY INTO ME. Of course he was! I'm blonde! I'm thin as a rail! I have professional landscaping done on my newly bought home! A holy old pug died due to my fuckup!

Unfortunately, just as he was getting more and more interested, I was starting to feel more and more mentally unhinged, increasingly frightened, because I couldn't feel "ME." I wasn't able to calm down, my thoughts running up an endless circular staircase. I was angsty, angry anxiety.

But no worries! He's PERFECT!! Did I mention he wrote sitcoms? That he owned two homes? That he had three lovely grown kids whom he introduced to me VERY CASUALLY OVER SKYPE when I was traveling in Singapore? And THIS PERFECT GUY SAYS HE LOVES ME. It's just a month in, so it's fast. Did I mention he's from WINNIPEG? WINNIPEG COULD NOT BE MORE IDEAL. It makes all the sense.

NO RED FLAGS HERE! (I, of course, have many red flags. They are performed in my stand-up act for all to see. He probably just didn't watch my stuff, or maybe his critical listening skills were muted in the sound buffer of my thick blonde mane.)

It was immediate, all-in enthusiasm, because that's how falling in love works! That's when you know it's Velveteen Rabbit Real.

Okay, he did shit-talk his ex-wife. Which makes sense! She's your ex-wife! My God, you love/loved each other and had three children! I get it! But ten years later, after divorcing, you're still mad? And angry about money? But you're rich. Huh. Anyhoo, it's cool! That's not a bad sign, because HE LOVES ME. And I am not HER!

And we talked about mental illness! He had experienced depression in the form of writer's block. He went for help to a writing coach. The coach helped him get back to writing again and now he felt fine. Well, that's great! Oh! And his mother had been hospitalized for depression.

`ME: That's great that she took care of herself.`

[*Silence.*]

`WINNIPEG: I thought her attempting suicide was really selfish.`

He explained to me that he was still very angry at his mom for trying to kill herself and then for spending a few months in a psych ward to get herself together.

NOTE TAKEN! Now let's get back to talking about how pretty and talented I am, because this lack of compassion for your mother is definitely killing the mood!

But he's in love and I'm in love too? Like I can't believe it? This is Wyden Muskrat all over again. I've never had such a handsome, stable, shiny, BMW-driving person fall in love with me. I've always been the one who attracts ninety-day-sober alcoholics with anger-management problems, and men who have recently lost a hundred pounds and need support buying sweaters. Was it too good to be true? YES!

Two months into Our Love Story—half of which was via email—we had sex for the first time at one of the two homes he owned and complained about.

Sex in house number two went poorly and it was not the fault of the house. (He spoke with regret about a million-dollar house that he once had but sold in the divorce and how much it would be worth now and that he doesn't think his wife needs as much as she says she does. . . . OY. Dude, YOU HAVE TWO [2] FUCKING HOUSES, YOU HAVE KIDS, YOU HAVE A JOB, I yelled at him, with my laser eyes.) And with ragging on his once-beloved wife as foreplay, it all fizzled. He lost interest halfway through, and I shook like a plastic bag on barbed wire. Sometimes the vagine shuts down when someone is frustrated with it not being a raging-waters ball pit for his pleasure. That's what happened with me and Mr. Perfect. I was nervous, and I guess that's not sexy. He drove me home silently in the BMW.

The vibe changed. I was no longer a strong, independent, sexy woman. I was now another goddamned bitch of a human being.

A few weeks later, I told him that I was going to go into the hospital to get some support in changing my meds to Lamictal. I tried to sell it: "It's like a dental checkup! Just getting my neurons a good floss and fluoride." Before I checked in, he asked me out for what I sensed was The Last Supper.

As the perfect guy he was/is, he drove over from Sherman Oaks to my house in Eagle Rock (props for driving thirty minutes to break up with me in person). We walked all the way (eight slow blocks) to a local restaurant. We ordered and ate a whole meal together, and this brave man (during my last forkful of Caesar salad) addressed the evening's agenda. He said, "Hey, this is a really bad time for me." Then we walked all eight blocks' way back to my house, wherein I tried to ask what a "bad time" meant, even though I knew it meant that I was the bad time.

My friend Amy, having met the guy, was ridiculously surprised. She said, "He said he loved you! He'll come back!" Oh no, Amy. He was not coming back.

And he didn't. And he is now married to a therapist. Hilarious.

I did what I told him I would do and went into the psych ward. I googled psych facilities in my zip code and came up with Las Encinas Hospital! And when your brain is collapsing, you find out who your friends are, by who sticks around and by whom you reach out to—which in my case was Amy, Marketa, my family, and some professional strangers.

And soon Amy picked me up in her Ford Flex and dropped me off at the hospital.

PART III

The Cult of Mental Health Care

17. Hospitalization #1

I take pleasure in plans. I love an itinerary, a laminated, bullet-pointed, cruise-director cheat sheet. Especially for a descent into madness. I chose a facility close to my home, emailed everyone that I'd be gone for three days, and got a ride from my pal Amy. She said I was talking too fast! Well then! Let's nip this in the bud! I wouldn't stop talking and I couldn't stop talking! I was just speaking what was going on in my head, which was an unending, nonstop loopdeloop of confused rage plus ideas without pause. It was a feeling that I had not had before, outside of panic attacks, which lost their power once I'd read about them. This was the panic attack feeling plus words, plus obsesh plus depresh (I've got to kill these thoughts by killing myself). When I hear that someone died by suicide because they "could not take it anymore," I think about the way I felt then. Though all I looked like was probably a little hyper and weepy, I felt BAAAAAAAAAAAAAAAAAAAAAD. If you've been in such a situation, you know what I mean. If you haven't, good for you.

I wanted to go in for the cure, one of those fast-acting psych meds I was always hearing about, and be out for a tight headlining set of stand-up comedy. It would be the responsible thing to do. The sane thing! No need to panic. I had this totally under control! I had *insurance*!

I really thought I could just get my meds taken care of before I had to do four shows in Chicago the next weekend, followed by five shows in Austin, Texas, followed by a voice-over, after an acting job, followed by another dream job into perpetuity! STAY ON SCHEDJ!

I was in high spirits. I packed pj's! A journal I wouldn't write in! A few outfits without strings to hang myself with! A swimsuit for the pool pictured on the website! Shoes without laces! Nothing to be ashamed of! I was going to take care of it myself! My psychiatrist had told me to try a med that would make me gain weight or that would slow me down. She told me to check myself into Glendale Adventist Medical Center, which didn't sound as pleasant as this Las Encinas Shangri-Spa. I was going to get the CUTTING-EDGE TREATMENT at a CUTTING-EDGE FACILITY and be CUTTING EDGES! NO THANK YOU, I'VE GOT THIS, DR. LINDA WOODALL!

My favorite thing about how dreadful psych facilities can be is that the marketing for them is the ultimate in gaslighting false advertising. In the case of Lost at Sea Hospital of LA, a gorgeous campus set amongst the trees with plenty of programs and facilities: "The finest care in the finest setting!" "Las Encinas" means "The Holm Oaks" in Spanish!

I had already been to many DA meetings in the hospital's community room, Sundays at 3 p.m., and so knew that the campus was, in fact, very pretty. There are tons of *encinas* and 1920s vintage buildings! If that doesn't sell you on this Hampton Inn for Mentals, there's yoga! And a pool! A pool? Where people are in danger of self-harm? Seems odd, but there it is in photos and words! And unlike Hilton Properties, they "take most insurances"! And if you're wondering what's going to be happening all day long while you're kicking benzos or coming down off that public dance in your birthday suit on your ex-husband's lawn, here is the schedule, which is STILL on their website and is, excepting mealtimes, a pack of lies.

7:00-7:30 am	Wake up
7:30-8:00 am	Breakfast
8:00-9:00 am	Yoga or Gym Time
9:00-10:00 am	Community Meeting
10:00-10:50 am	Seeking Safety with Dr. Christianson
11:00-12:30 pm	Men or Women's Process Group
12:30- 1:00 pm	Lunch
1:30- 2:30 pm	SMART Recovery
2:30-3:30 pm	Swimming and Recreation
4:00-5:00 pm	Mindfulness and Relapse Prevention
5:00-5:30 pm	Dinner
6:00-7:00 pm	Recovery Lecture
7:30-9:00 pm	On-site AA Meeting
9:00-9:30 pm	Community Wrap-up
9:30-10:45 pm	Fellowship, Program Assignments
11:00 pm	Lights Out

All of this sounded almost too good to be true! It is! None of it happens! You do get food and go to bed. And okay, there were meetings that were AA-flavored with some Kahlil Gibran digressions.

After chauffeuring me over in her Ford Flex, Amy waited with me in the fancy old lobby with silk flowers as I vibrated on a settee. Someone gave me a form to fill out and I did my best to get it all down there—maybe a thirty-minute process. When it was time for Amy to leave, a door opened to the clinical area. Sadly, Amy had already left when I was told that my insurance didn't cover care and that if I wanted to *stay* I would have to write a check (thank goodness I had checks! I'm a prepared traveler!) for three grand. Full disclosure: it is a sign of mania to spend insane amounts of money (especially on things you won't value when you come out of the episode). I wrote out the check for 3K.

As I was to find out, no matter how much you pay for them, most mental health facilities are fairly worn and dodgy. But it was surprising, after the alluring website, to see the worn, incomplete puzzles, the big-screen TV playing ultimate fighting championships at the loudest volume possible (remote was lost), and the orange plastic industrial smoke bucket under the one tree in a yard that was otherwise a small grassy area surrounded by chain-link fencing. *Through* the fencing you could see the beautiful grounds of the hospital . . . no longer accessible to patients due to insurance reasons. The pool was locked and drained. The schedule from the internet above was still posted on a wall, and when I very casually, through the gritted teeth of rictus, asked a nurse where everything on the schedule was happening, the bedraggled health professional said, "Oh, we don't do that anymore." Oh. Then, irritated with me, the madwoman, she further elucidated: "This is a hospital."

"I know. It's just the website and this wall say, 'Yoga. Swimming.'"

She repeated irritatedly, "This is a hospital." Okay. And I get it: this isn't a hotel. I'm not saying it's not a hospital. Although now that you're acting so defensive, I'm starting to worry: Is this just a rough Best Western in Monrovia?

My room was a little hot, but I didn't have any roommates and I had a nice view of an *encina* stump (the tree had been cut down for insurance reasons). This is where I might start to feel better. And I had so much work coming up. . . . I just wanted to get this medication change over and done with and get back to feeling like "myself."

I meandered into one of the twelvish-step groups that happened a few times a day. I met a lady who said she'd been diagnosed with bipolar I and used to have a full-time international-travel job. Now, because of the illness, she could only work part-time in a bead store. Oh my Christ. I wasn't able to work in a store BEFORE this meltdown. I'm not sure I could make it in the high-volume pressure cooker that is Bead Sales. I began panicking. I had a mortgage. All those beads! And then packaging them up for people and the chitchat and the disappointment on people's faces when we were out of red ones! EVERYONE LOVES THE BRIGHT RED BEAD. My new friend couldn't provide me with any advice, just that she was here in the hospital about once a year to regroup and her hubby was going to pick her up in a few days.

I tried to stay in contact with my "real" life. I even encouraged a sponsee, Nicole, to call me at my new temporary number (the psych ward wall phone).

MARIA: Hey, Nicole, just calling you back!

NICOLE: Where are you at?

MARIA: Oh, I'm in the hospital.

NICOLE: Oh no—what happened?

MARIA: Oh no, I'm fine. It's the psych ward.

NICOLE: You're in the psych ward?

MARIA: Yeah—just changing my meds . . .

[*Long pause.*]

NICOLE: Hey, maybe you shouldn't be sponsoring right now.

[*Shorter pause.*]

MARIA: Oh, yeah. Yes, maybe you're right.

NICOLE: I hope you feel better soon.

MARIA: Oh, thanks. Well, talk to you later!

NICOLE: Take care.

The meals, which were plentiful and on schedule, were all deep-fried cafeteria-style food, which of course is my favorite and Every Person's Favorite. French fries are a great strategy for weaning yourself off an opioid addiction, which many of my compatriots were doing. And who's going to want to go back to meth after gaining a hundred pounds eating onion rings? (From what I heard at the AA/NA meetings, almost everybody.)

The second day, not yet dimmed by greasy delights, I got to see a doctor—and this is true—his name was Dr. Pilz. Dr. Pilz is retired now, which is good.

And before I even got to see Dr. Pilz, I had to beg the overworked, exhausted nursing staff in their sealed glass box to give me back my purse. There was a lot of hemming and hawing until I told them I just had to get my checkbook out to pay Dr. Pilz $450 UP FRONT. DR. PILZ ONLY TAKES CASH. With a Dr. Pilz payment needed, a nurse threw my purse at me with the athleticism of a quarterback.

Okay. Sesh with Dr. Pilz.

Dr. Pilz, a chunky older guy, legs sprawled across the beat-up coffee table, toggling two cell phones (other patients he's texting with?). There was an open laptop on the coffee table in front of him. He took my check for $450 without a thank-you. He was busy. #grind

"So, why are you here?"

"Uh, I'm worried I'm going to kill myself. I'm changing meds and I don't feel good."

"Okay. Do you work?"

This is where I should have been more cagey. I could have said I was a bookkeeper, which I am sort of, but only with Quicken. (I let a professional named Mindy handle the QuickBooks.) Ill-advisedly, as I had full mentals, I said: "Comedian."

There are many jobs that get stressful responses from strangers. From what I've heard, these include doctor ("Could you take a look at this skin tag?"), therapist ("I was molested as an infant in my dream last night"), sex worker ("So how does it work, do you take PayPal?"), teacher ("WOW! That is so important. I could never do that. Or I could but I won't!"), and accountant ("Oh"). Comedian usually gets one of the following:

- Tell me a joke.
- Are you funny?
- My favorite comedian is ________.
- Have I seen you in anything?
- You don't seem like a comedian.

Thankfully, Dr. Pilz didn't say any of the above. He just continued typing on his laptop. A moment passed. I felt a motor running in reverse within my heart-mind. Then, shockingly, there was a woman's high voice coming from his laptop. He turned the screen around to face me.

"Is this you?"

Yes, it was me. It was a set I'd done on *Conan* from 1999.

"Uh-huh."

"You're funny."

WOW. I can understand maybe worrying I was in a grandiose state of psychosis claiming to be a comedian in LA County, but even if I say I'm Howie Mandel, wait till I leave the room to google my name. It's just polite.

Getting back to business, I explained to him that I had been acting odd and that my psychiatrist had suggested I might need a new medication, and also that I had shows coming up and I wanted to be ready for work. I also made it VERY clear that I didn't want to gain weight or be tired. No thank you! CUTTING EDGE, I tell you! Lamictal. EVERYBODY IS DOING WELL ON LAMICTAL!

With all of his interest in his job, I would think that Dr. Pilz might have taken a second to notice that sometimes the side effects of Lamictal are cognitive, making it difficult to think or talk. By the time I noticed on my own, a week later, I was on my way to Chicago for four shows.

Hooooo oooooon. Or should I say, OH NO.

PSYCH WARD MENU

No cooking for you!

And no vegetables either!

1. Your brain is fried and so everything you eat is deep fried. Tater Tots, potato skins, chicken tenders, yellow sheet cake—if you're off your rocker, they're trying to get you to calm down with some carbs.
2. The one thing that isn't made of gluten is coleslaw! You eat plates of slaw with the occasional granola bar, and you maintain your fighting weight because you've got shows to do in Chicago next weekend!
3. YOU'RE ON LAMICTAL AND NOTHING WILL SLOW YOU DOWN (EXCEPT, PERHAPS, LAMICTAL).

18. Hospitalization #2

I had been out from this Las Encinas hospital for a day and had just one more day to get my head together before traveling to Chicago. Despite my stay at the hospital and my new meds, I was very OFF. I did not feel any better and actually felt a lot worse. But I figured that was just temporary! Suck it up! Get support! I kept checking with friends, trying to calm myself down, getting assurance that they thought I could do the job. They all seemed very confident in my abilities.

I went to lunch in LA with two comics and I asked them if I seemed normal. My pal Joe Keyes said, "You're going to do great, as always!" This is the usual thing to say to any performer who is nervous, because if you've practiced and you've been doing something for over ten years, you're not likely to completely fall apart. This time, however, I couldn't get my brain to work for even one minute to rehearse the sixty minutes of material that I had done dozens of times before.

The fact that I couldn't even focus enough to rehearse should have been a warning sign that I should cancel the dates. But I kept at it, hoping it would get better—that maybe the next minute, hour, or the next day I'd be able to concentrate after a tall glass of milk. Maybe I'd be able to say the words over and over to myself so that they stuck, the way I had always done before. But the time to perform got closer, and I wasn't feeling any better. I hoped that muscle memory would take over. I hoped the acts of traveling, getting to the hotel, and following through with the gig would force me into feeling and being functional.

On the flight to Chicago, I had the mounting realization that I was making a mistake. I couldn't go through the material at all. This lack of prep (and this time I was practicing) had not happened since I botched a violin solo when I was sixteen. I checked into the hotel. In an effort to warm up for the show, I thought, "I'll go on a walk and run the set," something I'd done hundreds of times before.

I don't remember the walk exactly, but I panicked and stumbled around a neighborhood; I lost my driver's license, my credit card, and my hotel room key. I then managed to cut myself quite deeply on a taxi bumper. I could not SAY my jokes out loud. I was lost but then recognized a street, and I ran frantically back to the hotel. I didn't have any ID to get into my room, but I had just checked in and the clerk recognized me and could tell, I think, that I was having some sort of meltdown, and she let me back in. I started crying while also desperately trying to mouth my jokes aloud, which in retrospect is sort of hilarious. I kept stuttering. I called Bruce, my manager. Not making a whole lot of sense.

"BLLLLLOAAAAAAAARGH. HUCH," I said. "AAAA. AAAAAAA—I can't talk. BLRB."

Bruce was, as always, cool as a deep-baritone cucumber. "No problem," he told me. "I'll take care of it."

I called my mom.

"Maaaa!"

"Honey, somehow get to the airport," she said. "Go to the Delta desk. Tell them that you are *Gold Medallion*, and tell them about your website."

I somehow got a taxi driver to take a personal check for a ride to the airport. My mom was right: Delta WAS better than any health-care provider I've ever had. Airport security let me through (after a serious pat-down and double-checking of my name and address online) AND the flight attendant gave me a first-class upgrade, probably as much because my hand was bleeding and I was in tears as because I was a Gold Medallion member.

I got home, googled mental health hospitals in my zip code (that took my insurance, Blue Cross), drove myself to Glendale Adventist Medical Center, and checked in via the ER.

My psychiatrist's office is a block from the GAMC. Maybe now I'd get one of those mental health "teams" the National Alliance on Mental Illness is always talking about.

It took six hours—pretty fast, compared to LA County hospital (eight to twelve hours)—to be processed into the psych ward.

Although I was desperate to get help, I felt no relief once I was "in." I guess I believed that once I was admitted they would fix whatever was going wrong. But I felt no sense of camaraderie or healing. What I know now is that the psych ward is simply a place to be safe from yourself until the drugs kick in.

At this time, and during the three months to follow, I was closer to killing myself than I've ever been before or since. Every night I felt beyond grateful for the delivery of the meds that would knock me out of consciousness. I couldn't bear—I did not want to bear—being awake. I'd never felt this way before. I was given enough Xanax to pass out for eight hours at night.

Again, my psychiatrist, when I checked into Glendale Adventist, suggested Depakote. But, as I was mental, I still refused to go on Depakote, the seizure med and mood stabilizer that my mom had taken for thirty-five years. Why? Because one of the side effects was weight gain. Though I had experienced "recovery" from an eating disorder, I have never been free of the idea that it's acceptable for me to weigh over 130 pounds—or whatever arbitrary number I happen to have set for myself.

After those first seventy-two hours, I thought, "Well, that's enough. I should be better by now." And I entered the intensive outpatient treatment program. The program was five days a week, 10 a.m. to 3 p.m., all spent in groups. The groups were allegedly differentiated by topic:

COGNITIVE BEHAVIORAL: Therapist plays a gonging noise and then people share about whatever crisis they're currently in (which is being in an intensive outpatient treatment program for mental illness). Gong!

BACK-TO-WORK SKILLS: Another therapist reads an Oprah quote and then people share about whatever crisis they're currently in (which is being in an intensive outpatient treatment program for mental illness). We close with the Serenity Prayer.

HEY, STOP IT or ADDICTIONS: The first therapist comes back and tells us to shake out our bodies from sitting so long in what will be the third hour of the group. Then people share about whatever crisis they're currently in (which is being in an intensive outpatient treatment program for mental illness). Break for Seventh-day Adventist vegetarian food for lunch.

It was healing to be with other people, I guess. But there was no vision for the future, no action plan, no "call each other and keep in touch!" Just sitting and listening to everyone's static stories over and over again. There were no goals, no exercises, no assignments, simply a purgatory of listening to everyone describe their fears.

Half the group members were first-time mental-health-care users. The other half were people who had been hospitalized several if not tens of times.

It was a very nice, worn-down holding tank/adult-day-care center.

The only thing I specifically remember a therapist saying to me was, "Hey, Maria. Can I talk to you?"

Sure.

We sit on a bench away in the hallway.

```
THERAPIST [whispering]: I just needed to tell
    you that I know you. Or, I know who you are.
    I have friends who are comedians.
MARIA: Oh.
THERAPIST [still whispering]: I always go to the
    Comedy Store. Do you go up there? I've never
    seen you there. They must have an auditioning
    process. Great club.
MARIA: Uh-huh.
THERAPIST [whisper-whisper]: Anyway, I just
    wanted to let you know that I would never
    tell ANYBODY that I saw you here.
MARIA: Okay.
```

Later I wrote a joke in which I set this conversation on the psych ward. In the joke, my response was: "I'm in a county-stamped gown with electric-green gripper socks that are not my own. So you tell whoever the fuck you want. ALL IS LOST."

At the time, I just walked away.

Beyond gritting my teeth through each waking hour, there are two other elements of treatment I remember well. The first is yellow sheet cake. EVERY DAY. A big brick of cuckoo cake with frosty-white frosting. Slide on a durable plastic plate and serve it to all. The second element is a purple van ride to and from home (due to the danger of driving on new meds).

Those five weeks were abysmal. I was alive, but I still didn't feel safe. I WAS safe from hurting myself (which still felt like a good option) during the day for a few hours, and I was at least with people I didn't have to pretend with. Yet there was no one—including the therapists—who could say, simply: "You're going to get better," as I think they don't really know either. Everybody *wants* you to get better, but they don't know what medication is going to work. I think that's like most illnesses/school courses/human relationships. No one can guarantee security and stability, which is a real bummer when you think about it. Don't think about it.

The purple van would pick me up from my house in the morning and then drop me off in the late afternoon.

My favorite memory is of riding home in the van and at a point one minute before passing their eyeglass store, Society of the Spectacle, I'd text my pals Amy and Katie (the owners). Amy and Katie O'Connell are sisters, and my close friends, along with Marketa, who are DOWN for mental health crisis. I have several friends, but you kind of know who is going to be able to better handle certain situations. I'd text Amy and Katie, "Purple van in 60 seconds!" and if they weren't with customers, both of them would come to their store barn door and lean out the top window, waving and yelling, "HI, MARIA!" as I waved from the back of the packed purple van filled with my meds-sodden compatriots. Whisking past, I'd be dropped off at home, and I'd fall in a heap. If I had the energy, sometimes we'd all go out for dinner, and I remember one time Amy having to pull my head up out of my salad when some combination of benzos and mood stabilizers put me to sleep in the appetizer.

There is so much joyous gratitude I have—IN RETROSPECT—for this horrible time. And the key word is "time." These friends took TIME. Every day I was in the psych ward, either Amy, Marketa, or Katie, or all three, would show up during visiting hours (they all had full-time jobs) and would bring me Diet Coke in plastic bottles and gas station chocolate and generally try to converse with my blank face while surrounded by the mummering-sadness of a psych ward: rubber curtains, loud TV, security doors, moaning, yelling, and bird calls. They were THERE EVERY DAY. And every day—for a total of what I think over that year was about sixteen days—is a lot. Especially in Los Angeles.

If you have ever lived in LA, then you know that to do anything in LA, to go anywhere, takes forty-five minutes. So, let's say you want to get together with someone for lunch—that's going to average almost three hours out of your day. If you are going anywhere at rush hour, then that is the only place you are going today. For two weeks of days, these LA friends made an LA road trip to see me, their only trip that day. I realize, as I'm writing this, that I should reimburse Marketa and Amy and Katie for gas money. They gave me one of the best gifts I've ever received, which is, at a time I was in no way useful or fun to be around, their attention, presence, and tolerance when I was at my worst, without the promise that I'd get better.

I want to reiterate that I did not have hope. My brain was incapable of thinking, "This will pass," or, "The right medication might help." My brain was completely unavailable for any sort of Norman Vincent Peale nonsense.

About a week after being out of that first outpatient eight-week program, I had a few jobs set up: relatively short-term voice-over roles and tiny TV sketch scenes, which meant I didn't have to keep it together for too long, maybe four hours at a time. It felt abhorrent. Like there was no way I could do it.

Dr. Woodall again recommended Depakote. Nope. So then she said, "Let's take you off all your medication and then do a brain scan and see what medication your brain might respond best to."

I don't know what kind of science this was based on, but I did it, feeling wildly hopeless. Like WOW bad. She jellied some paper discs attached to wires on my head and took readings and the results, surprise, were: I'd do well on Depakote. The medication she'd been trying to get me on in the first place but that I kept refusing because I didn't want to gain weight. At this point, I felt so abominable that even my weird eating disorder ego was outgunned. I said, okay, I'll take it.

SO I began taking the Depakote, but it was a little too late to avoid just one more in-patient hospitalization.

It was just one day after going on Depakote: I was on my second round of outpatient day-program treatment, and I had an appointment with the therapist. She asked me, "Are you safe to go home by yourself today?"

And I paused.

I had five bottles of pills of all different kinds that I was keeping on the kitchen counter at the time. A very humorous part of mental health care is how many meds they allow you to procure and hoard, through all the changes and fluctuations in pharmaceutical dosages, unobserved at home. Everyone has established on paper that you're not thinking right, and then they send you home with bottle after bottle of Alice in Wonderland! I had plenty: three different kinds of benzos, antidepressants, an antipsychotic, and now Depakote!

I said, "Well . . ."

She wouldn't let me leave and called for a wheelchair (for insurance reasons), and I was wheeled back into Psych West for my third and, I hoped, final stay.

RECIPE FOR PSYCH WARD GRAHAM CRACKERS

1. Knock on the window of the nurses' station.
2. No one will look up. There are three people in there, on computers or chatting.
3. Knock again.
4. No one will make eye contact, but one nurse will turn her body toward you to acknowledge your presence.
5. The nurse will then apologize to the person they're talking to in order to look at you, while still keeping her conversation going.
6. Say: "Uh. I was just seeing. Somebody said you had graham crackers up here."
7. She reaches in a drawer, for a single pack of two generic-brand graham crackers.
8. You thank her profusely, but she doesn't notice, because she has already turned away.
9. Unwrap and eat without liquid, mouthing, "THIS IS A HOSPITAL, NOT A HOTEL. THIS IS A HOSPITAL, NOT A HOTEL." In case you were feeling at all confused about where you were.

19. Hospitalization #3: Certificate of Completion

This round in, like the punch line in the rule of three, was the kicker. I felt worse than ever and didn't have any faith that Depakote would work, though I hadn't taken any action toward my suicidal ideation. When I say that I felt bad, it's as if my mind/body had become a vibrating razor blade of electric psychic pain. I had no moment that I felt okay—my greatest wish would be to be knocked out by a professional baseball pitch to the temple. But at least now I had given up and gone on the drugs Dr. Woodall had suggested in the first place. I was finally on what is my current prescription of 1,000 mg of Depakote, 50 mg of Seroquel, and 40 mg of Prozac, but it hadn't yet gotten into my system.

I went into the hospital on a Thursday, which meant I had to check in with the weekend psychiatrist, who I now wonder maybe isn't as good as other psychs and therefore needs to take the undesirable weekend shift. The doctor was an irritable man with an accent that I believe was Armenian. I was weakly glad, because the one other Armenian psych I'd seen had been WONDERFUL.

Before the Weekend Armenian Doctor, there had been the Weekday Armenian Doctor. That doctor, Dr. Weekday Marfazian, had sat down (at a considerate distance) on my bed and said to a psychiatric patient in the midst of mentals—I shit you not—"Tell me everything from the beginning."

And I did! And Dr. M seemed interested (which is either very good acting or he is a fantastic human being, either reason being useful). I tried to see this magical Dr. Marfazian later outside the hospital, but he didn't take insurance, and though I "value" myself, I also "value" not spending three hundred dollars an hour when all I need is a meds check. I am probably wrong to be so cheap with my own health, but I feel like a yearly pair of clogs takes the edge off more than an amazing bedside manner.

And now back to my second doctor of Armenian descent. Like any racist, I assumed his personality was just like Dr. Marfazian's. Thinking he was just like Marfazian, I gave this new guy the story from the very beginning without him even asking for it! I'm sure I said it quickly and agitatedly with a little grimace every few seconds, because that was my style at the time. I started with the problems I had as a nine-year-old—not being able to sleep, the intrusive-thought OCD—and was going to move into my teenage years when

BZHISHK SHIT'HED: I've never heard of that.

ME: Oh yes! It's a type of OCD called intrusive thoughts. It's that I have an obsessional fear that I'm going to act out violently or sexually against other people.

That's when I really fucked myself over. I decided I had nothing to lose and was on my way out of the world possibly anyways, so who cares—and it was my job to EDUCATE Bzhishk Shit'hed about harm from OCD (urgently trying to EDUCATE people about something can be a sign of mania!).

BZHISHK SHIT'HED: That is psychosis.

ME [*rushed speech of a mental*]: No, it's not. I mean, psychosis is fine and it's definitely a symptom of mental illness, but harm OCD is the FEAR that you MIGHT do something that you desperately don't want to do. It is not doing something in a state of unreality, nor is it sociopathy, where there is a desire and pleasure in harming a person, place, or thing (which also, frankly, deserves some sort of treatment better than prison)!

BZHISHK SHIT'HED: You are psychotic. I'm going to put you on a ten-day mandatory hold.

ME: What? No, I'm trying to tell you that I'm actually afraid of hurting/desperately don't *want* to and have NEVER hurt anyone physically or sexually (unless you count poor blow-job technique, which you'd really have to go back a few years to find).

BZHISHK SHIT'HED: [*Walks away to do ten-day-hold paperwork.*]

I felt so bad anyway that I didn't really care, and I couldn't get my thoughts together to argue, and really, the more you advocate for yourself in a psych ward, the more mental they think you are. I tried to write out a bunch of book recommendations about OCD for Bzhishk Shit'hed and leave it at the nurses' station, but I very much doubt he sat down and read a torn piece of paper with the tiny pencil block letters in the shape of a spiral rectangle.

I stood in line for my package of graham crackers at 8 p.m., got my Xanax, and settled in for ten more days.

I attended the groups. These groups had rough themes, but the themes seemed beyond everyone's current abilities to comprehend. There was a "movement" group. I joined in, but it was *seated* movement group and I was too anxious to sit, so I crouched in the corner. The therapist in charge, who had long hair and played Cat Stevens's "Moonshadow" over a tinny boom box, said that unless I sat down, I couldn't be in the group. I told her I felt anxious and that I had a lot of energy in my legs. Would it be okay to do the Running Man in place? No? Cool. I'll sit and clench my buttocks together.

There was arts and crafts, where we were taken into a room with paper and markers. Some of the paper had outlines of flowers or other patterns you could fill in. There were some dusty computers in a corner. In that same room, we had a self-care group in which they would wheel in a tray of very old ninety-nine-cent-store makeup and grooming products, and we would get to "sign out" a lipstick. There were no mirrors available (cutting hazard), so you had to use the dusty computer screens as a reflection to estimate where to apply the ancient orangey wax on your lips. In a better time, I would have put a circle on each cheek, but I regret to report that during this period a lot of comedic opportunities passed me by.

The most passionate and unhinged therapist was an older white guy with a beard who opened each group with a Buddhist perspective: "Hey, guys, life is suffering. Discuss!" He was preaching to the choir. He would start each session by going around the group, asking each of us, "So, how are you feeling today?"

PATIENT 1: Depressed. I want to kill myself.

THERAPIST: Okay, thanks for sharing. And you?

PATIENT 2: I have a television in my chest.

THERAPIST: Glad you're here. And you?

PATIENT 3: [*No response*.]

After going around the circle, he would then launch into some of the most inappropriate spiritual monologues I've ever wanted to heckle:

"The Buddha says the root of all pain is craving. That is the *dhukka*. There are three types of suffering: the suffering of suffering, the suffering of change, and the suffering of existence."

BOOOOOOOOOOOOOOOOOO! Wrong crowd, buddy. Great material, wrong crowd.

Ultimately, in-patient hospitalization, just like my twelve-step groups, was in no way transformative for me at this time, aside from providing somewhere to go during the day. I wasn't really "there." If you are not "there," it's difficult to be a part of anything. It was like if you were in the end stages of inoperable cancer and someone said, "Well, we can't do anything about the pain, but we can sit you up in a log flume ride with other people in the end stages of inoperable cancer!" A log flume may have provided an element of refreshing water and a terrified camaraderie. I don't NOT recommend a log flume ride.

My sister, Sarah, visited me. She brought a life coach friend and did a chakra-healing thing on my head right in my hospital room.

The chakra ceremony involved bells and an oil. I don't believe in those processes, but I do believe that human beings attempting to love and care for each other is mostly positive, so sign me up for whatevzsh.

Later, my sister would assert that the ceremony was what cured my bipolar episode, rather than the medical medicines coursing through my veins. She knows I totally disagree with that. I tell myself that the reason I get work as a comedian is a result of hard work and tenacity (and hundreds of years of privilege, an easy-street childhood, and a shocking amount of luck), but it could genuinely just be because I have a high voice and a clown angel watches over me from clown heaven. That said, I'm going to keep swallowing my pills with a bump of Diet Coke.

After my third hospitalization, and first eight-week round of outpatient treatment, I did feel "better." And when I say "better," I mean that after getting out of the hospital for the third time, I went through the exact same eight-week outpatient treatment program of sitting around in circles of people like me. Near the end of this eight weeks of outpatient treatment, I was able to think. Not well, but I was able to think about trying to think, which is pretty close to thinking and less vibrating like a tuning fork.

Meds have changed my life. In a deep and what feels like a lasting way, they have allowed me to maintain what I understand now to be a "baseline" mood. I don't feel high, but I also don't feel really low (unless I have an alcoholic beverage I'm not supposed to have). And here's the kicker: I still want to stop taking meds. For this book—over what are the now three years I've been writing it—at least twice, I've cut my meds to 500 mg to have more "energy."

Unfortunately, what immediately follows cutting the drugs is me going back to feeling at first great and then, quickly, ampedly, angrily unstable.

20. BOUNDARIES: I WILL NOT JOIN *JUST* ANYTHING

I've heard great things about Tony Robbins, but it's too flash for my spending plan AND I already watched his documentary. He is physically terrifying, but not due to his height. He screams at people on a microphone from a high stage about their very personal issues. Also, the crowds are too large. I don't want to be a part of a movement that is AT ALL popular. But I will give most belief systems a solid attempt. Unitarianism, Marie Kondo, and anything that will get me going in a fresh way, put me on the email list. But sometimes you find a "life-changing new lifestyle" that is in no way helpful and must be either thrown in the trash or left responsibly in a Little Free Library that's low on nonfiction titles.

I just want to provide a cautionary note about the following tome that I felt ashamed didn't work for me. And that is what cults always say if you end up not being into it: "You're afraid/you're just not willing to really commit to yourself (yet!)." Those fuckers. The added pressure of being offered this kind of help when you really need help is that you feel doubly bad when it doesn't work for you.

The book I'm talking about is called *Ten Days to Self-Esteem*, by David Burns.

It is a 1970s-era telephone book–size workbook that requires the levels of discipline and concentration of a decorated astronaut. There were hundreds of copies of this book at the Glendale Adventist psych hospital. Someone (DAVID BURNS, perhaps?) must have donated them, because this book was insane.

I am voraciously supportive of all creative efforts, to the extent that I'll even acknowledge the craft involved in hate speech. "Bitches ain't shit" isn't NOT grammatically tenable and packs a punch.

I generally don't allow myself a "preference" for one TV show over another—at least not in the company of strangers. This is because it is difficult for me even to get up in the morning, let alone to take a pass at a short story, open a box of crayons, or spell-check a chapter of this book. To express hardened, definitive criticism of someone else's project feels hypocritical, like a sad comedian taking a swipe at a helpful, educated professional with well-honed instincts and ideas. When I say that I dislike a piece of writing, please know that I am fighting an ingrained personality trait that has even looked for the positive in the wildly creative spelling of trolls.

Ten Days to Self-Esteem by Dr. David Burns, MD, is hands down one of the most ludicrous exercises in self-help that has ever been given to me for free from a psychiatric program. It is also the only book I've ever been given for free from a therapist, so maybe I should be more grateful. Though not a cult that I fell for, it deserves at least a page of discussion as an homage to all the subjectively ill-fitting, useless, time-wasting, burdensome treatments that people with psychiatric problems invariably experience on the road to getting help that works for them.

Ten Days to Self-Esteem is filled with ornate word-puzzle exercises printed in eight-point font. Dr. Burns has that irritating, obnoxious tone, employed by many self-help leaders, that suggests that if you don't do the exercises, if you don't really do them PROPERLY, then maybe you didn't really want to improve in the first place. Maybe you don't really want to FEEL GOOD. You bastard. Dr. Burns is a professor at both Stanford and Harvard, which only bolsters my argument that his tone is condescending.

The pseudo-science of the book, which is backed up by actual science that I won't read, is as follows:

> You feel the way you think. Bad feelings come from bad thoughts. Therefore, you can change the way you feel from bad to good by changing your thoughts from bad thoughts to good thoughts.

But of course! That makes sense! Just change your thoughts!

If you're feeling well enough to answer even one of the questions out of the thousands that fill this goddamned MCAT prep of worksheets, you're not depressed. You might feel down, but you've got some bandwidth and you're able to appreciate the minute shades of difference between thinking "I AM a mistake" and "I MADE a mistake."

The highly stressful, detail-oriented thing you're supposed to do in this book—at the same time that you're thinking about killing yourself all day long—is to log in a SIX-COLUMN SQUARE your personalized experiences of "cognitive distortions." For example:

- All-or-nothing thinking. **This book sucks.**
- Overgeneralizing. **This book, like everything in life, sucks.**
- Mental filter. **All I have in life is this free fucking book.**
- Discounting the positives. **Even burning this book doesn't mean that there wouldn't be more copies of this book.**
- Magnification. **This book will kill me before I kill myself.**
- Mind-reading. **The guy who wrote this book knew I would hate it.**
- Fortune-telling. **I know I won't complete even the first page of this book.**
- Emotional reasoning. **I hate this book. Ergo, I hate this book.**

- "Should" statements. **I should be grateful for this noxious book that is free.**
- Labeling. **I hate *this* book, and so *I hate all books.***
- Self-blame. **It's all MY fault that I'm here in the loony bin stuck filling out this book that was some shady pay-to-play deal struck with the Seventh-Day Adventists by David Burns, MD.**
- Blaming others. **GODDAMN YOU, BURNS.**

BTW, this book has more than 1,500 five-star ratings on the internet monopolist bookseller sites. Everybody but me and one other guy loves it. I'm obviously wrong. But if you say I'm wrong about not liking this book and other subjective dislikes I have (e.g., watermelon Jolly Ranchers), go ahead and fill out this chart outlining the evidence that I'm wrong. Please do this task in the format of a DAILY MOOD LOG:

DESCRIBE YOUR FEELINGS

Record your negative feelings in PERCENTAGES (!!!) of 0–100%. Be specific. Is it really 34% of you that disagrees with me or is it 92%? What is the difference in feeling those two numbers in your body?

What you think I'm wrong about	How you might be wrong that I'm wrong	Percentage of how much you believe that this book is GREAT	The evidence of why it is GREAT. I'll need 10–119 examples.

Before you begin, I'd like you to write "YES" in this box that you are willing to do the work: [ ]

Now, write "YES" again, if you are truly going to do the work and aren't conning me: [ ]

Then, if you lied the first two times—write the percentage chance (0–100%) that you will fill out an *Oxford English Dictionary*'s worth of mental Mad Libs in ten days: [ ]

If you loved the David Burns books, may I judgmentally suggest that you may have a problem with anxiety or completist OCD, and, as a non-therapist, I advise you to throw your beloved Burns books into a body of water and tolerate the feelings that come up.

21. Bipolar Acting Job: *Lady Dynamite*

Around one year after stabilizing from my third hospital stay, a weird thing happened. Right when I was really bored with telling my own story, someone else became excited to tell it.

That person was Mitch Hurwitz, a seasoned TV producer and one of those unbelievably energetic and smart people who blow my mind with their relaxed extroversion and improvisation and effortless big-picture thinking. Years earlier, Mitch had heard my comedy albums and hired me to play DeBrie on *Arrested Development*. He had a deal with Netflix to make TV shows and was looking for possible collaborators.

I had been through the development process so many times before that I assumed nothing would happen beyond pleasant outdoor lunches (free!) on the Westside of LA. But Mitch kept wanting to move forward with the project, even though months passed when I didn't hear from him, since he had so many other obligations. I think going "mad" and losing EVERYTHING can be people's worst fear AND greatest wish, and I wonder if the story was interesting for that very reason? Action, cut, and print!

Because I had been through the process before, I was fairly relaxed. Due to my fairly recent loss of mind, I genuinely did not care. Meeting the suited professionals of Netflix, I actually ended up talking to one lady about how they were scared they were going to lose their home in Malibu because they had gotten themselves in a financial pickle and still wanted to send their kids to a private school. I told them about Debtors Anonymous and they laughed and I got a FREE bottle of water. A victory for all!

I remember getting my first acting job post-bananapants. I don't get acting jobs very often, but this time I got a small part on a Comedy Central sketch show with Nick Kroll. I had one line playing a pathetic eccentric woman hoarding pugs. I was to cry "My babies!" as I spread peanut butter all over my face and got attacked by non-stunt pugs, though union-repped pugs. Despite just being out of the pokey, I felt fairly certain that I was born to play a pathetic eccentric woman smearing her face with peanut butter. In the dressing trailer, my hands were tremoring, which, along with the nerves, created a sort of allover Magic Fingers Massage chair of my body. "My babies! [BEAT.] Smear peanut butter on face," I mumbled, practicing to myself over and over again. I was called to set and Nick was very nice and funny. I focused on The Work. "My babies!" SMEAR PEANUT BUTTER ON FACE. I had that familiar feeling that I almost always feel while acting, which is, "Can everybody see that I'm bad at this? That I'm in no way confident or comfortable and in fact may fuck up the entire production with my presence?" Action: "MY BABIES!" [*Beat.*] She smears peanut butter on her face, pugs attack her with kisses. It's ONE-TAKE BAMFORD!

HEY, MARIA! HOLD ON! YOU SKIPPED IT! SO HOW'D YOU MEET SCOTT? ONLINE! ABOUT A YEAR AFTER I LEFT THE PSYCH WARD! HE WAS FINE WITH MY BIPOLAR AND SAID IF I HAD TO GO IN AGAIN, HE'D COME IN AND SHAVE MY BEARD!

Around a year after getting out of the holding tank, I met Scott and in tandem, along with these development Caesar salads with Mitch Hurwitz, we moved forward, and before the filming of the first season, we were engaged. It was weird that Scott and I got together and then I got a TV show, because I had always thought it would be the opposite—that your dreams come true when you are beholden to no one, gloriously and powerfully alone. Instead, Scott's presence in my life made my mind open to "maybe I can do this" and that even if I failed in a huge way, he would have my back so why not give it a shot? Scott Marvel Cassidy was the main reason I was able to do *Lady Dynamite*, and I cannot underestimate how much his love and support made it possible for me to even try.

For whatever reason, Mitch had the wherewithal, genius, and vision to create a show I hoped I could do? I wasn't at all certain, but it wasn't a done deal anyway, so may as well keep going to the Westside for free food! As for my mental state, for around a year and a half after the final outpatient program, I was used to a nightly menu of 1,000 mg Depakote, 50 mg Seroquel, 40 mg Prozac.*

This meant I was sort of back to normal: able to do stand-up (with a little shake), but very sleepy except within five minutes of consuming cold brew coffee. Mitch gave me the wonderfully vague title of executive producer, which can literally mean anything or nothing; you can be a giant king-maker queen or a shadow. I chose shadow. My role carried

---

* FOR ANYONE INTERESTED: DRUGS I HAVE TAKEN

Psych meds I am sure that I have taken and their side effects:

- *Prozac:* less sexy times (some pain with intercourse)
- *Remeron:* dizzy, could not walk or drive (though I drove and walked to work)
- *Lamictal:* cognitive difficulties with articulation, thought (couldn't work)
- *Xanax:* sleepies (header into a salad)
- *Seroquel:* muscle weakness, weight gain, sleepiness (ongoing love affair! Yay, guaranteed sleep!)
- *Depakote*: tremor, weight gain, sleepiness (oh well!)
- *Wellbutrin:* COULD NOT STOP TALKING (lost weight but felt involuntarily extroverted)

Psych meds that sound familiar and I THINK I've tried, but I am not sure as I felt out of it at the time. I had about a dozen bottles of meds that I was prescribed

limited responsibilities of showing up, eating kale Caesar salads, and drinking pallets of lemon LaCroix. I didn't look ahead except to the crushed can of sparkling water in front of me. I was pretty sure I didn't have the energy to be the star of a show. I had read Patty Duke's biography: she was unmedicated during the peaks of her career and so a manic workhorse.

Sometimes employers—*before* you start the job—will be very accommodating. Oh yes, we know you're a parent! We know you need the weekends off! WORK-LIFE BALANCE! We are fully conscious of the limits of human existence! HAHAHA! We're going to be better than all the rest! We're a family and a family company. This [McDonald's/junta/feminist bookshop] is going to be different from all the others. Why? Because we're *listening*. We understand that great business and great products are made by healthy, happy people. *Si se puede!*

When the producers of the TV show assured me that any of my limitations would be accommodated, they were giving what is known as "lip service." I'm familiar with the maneuver, since I have used it numerous times with my loved ones. "Yes, I know I hurt your feelings with that joke, but I think you'll find if you just let me make the joke and hear people laugh, that you'll get that it's not about you, it's about all of us! My

---

during the Year of Mentals. Some I only took for one day because the side effects were so bad, but I can't remember what they all were. I know I got lots of comfort at the time from a website called www.crazymeds.com, where peers came together and talked about all the terrifying side effects, which are mostly terrifying because your brain is busted in the first place:

- *Tegretol: ?*
- *Ambien:* sleepies
- *Zoloft:* ?
- *Celexa:* ?
- *Klonopin: ?*
- *Abilify:* ?
- *Zyprexa:* ?

I see the ads out for new stuff today, sad actors with paper-plate smiley faces over their real, sad faces, and I assume I could try many, many more options. But I will not. The current meds work well enough and that is—as they say—something.

withering, bone-chilling, dead-on impersonation of you is really about humanity!"

The subject of the TV show was my own mental illness. So naturally, there was a lot of very concerned, very sincere talk about reasonable hours.

"Hey, we can't have you going mental when the show is about you trying not to go mental anymore! Ho-ho-ho!"

One of my favorite early suggestions was to do a "European shoot." This means eight hours of continuous filming followed by a break for, I guess . . . dinner and wine, Serge Gainsbourg karaoke?

I knew that a French-style, ten-to-six workday with lots of time for smoking and slowly sipped espresso was farfetched, but I harbored some hope that everyone understood that with the meds I was on, I was going to be struggling and needed to get enough sleep to prevent getting symptomatic/mental. In my mind (which we all know is faulty), we, the producers, agreed that however long the days, I would receive the Screen Actors Guild–mandated minimum turnaround time—the period between set departure and set arrival—of twelve hours.

There were five producers on the show, and three of those titles were ceremonial. Wonderful Mitch Hurwitz and magnificent Pam Brady were the truly active producers. Pam, a dear friend and colleague of Mitch's for many years, has a cattle dog—and that is her personality. DELIGHTED to wrangle people and ideas. She's totally weird and has an obsession with blow jobs. She is also an extremely functional person. There is a reason people get to the top of their professions. Pam is easy to be around, cheerful, and in no way moody. She also was down to energetically extrapolate on a story that I had told a million times and had no more real ideas about.

Pam was the real force behind the show, not only producing but writing and directing. She had the longest days: development, heading the writing room, editing, and watching me in person and on-screen via dailies for sixteen to twenty hours at a stretch—basically watching me do a janky job of bringing to life what she had written so beautifully. I don't think that even in my zippiest times of hypomanic productivity I could accomplish the kind of huge, extroverted leadership job that is TV production. I can do benign figurehead from a distance. I am very good at coming onto set occasionally to wave at everyone, eat a donut, and go back to my cave to desperately memorize lines.

As I said: there's the preproduction hope for change, and then there's the machine. The machine started up, and aside from the five poohbahs—Mitch, Pam, Bruce Smith, one person at Netflix, and me—I think everyone just forgot about my delicate-flower status and the twelve-hour-turnaround guarantee. The first day of shooting started and it was immediately, "Oh no! We're already behind schedule!"

What?

I felt agonized. It seemed like it was really bumming people out that I was going to stick to the twelve-hour turnaround. At the same time, just as I had predicted to Scott and close friends, I was already dying on my feet. I don't know if you've been on antipsychotics, but they really knock you out. It's like starting the day with an overdose of Benadryl, and then you're given more Benadryl as the day progresses, along with Diet Cokes to keep you awake, and just when you feel like you're going to pass out, you pop a cold brew and another Benadryl and keep going for eight more hours.

ASSHOLE: Oh, but Maria, see! There's your mistake. You must be on the wrong meds! Or you were overmedicated. Why didn't you get that fixed before the production?

ME: Oh, I'm sorry. Have you ever been on any medication for a chronic illness and found one that sort of works and felt terrified to change it? No? The last time I tried to cut my meds, I wrote half of a comedy album in one night. If you listened to the last one, you can be the judge of whether I should cut down on my meds regularly.

ASSHOLE: Did you try Wildly Untested New Drug, Unavailable Celebrity On-Call Health Professional, or New Age Ritual That's on a Yacht? This is important! A TV show! You should have done everything you could to be AT THE TOP OF YOUR GAME!

ME: YES, of course I tried EVERYTHING to make sure I was functioning well and doing a good job before this dream job, but also the only reason I had the dream job was because I have the mentals. You can't have both!

ASSHOLE: I'm just saying you could have done more. Like Famous Bipolar Person is bipolar and they have thirty-ten thousand shows around the Milky Way and are always cheerful, and I just saw them land a triple-toe sandman loop on Broadway AND they remembered my name!

ME: I know.

ASSHOLE: Just so you know.

"We've had a fifteen-hour day but you have to come back in ten hours so we can make up time! Otherwise, we're going over budget." I wish I was a productive producer's dream. For someone with more willingness (ambition) to just get it done, this would not have been a problem. I felt ashamed that I had to say, "Uh, remember how we said I was guaranteed by my union a twelve-hour turnaround?"

Painful silence. Confused hubbub of production staff.

I have friends who use wheelchairs who can tell countless stories of invitations and contracts to perform that end with them arriving at the venue only to find that they have no way to get inside the building, much less on the stage. You can't just manhandle a $75,000 wheelchair up the stairs to a black-box theater. So remember: if you invite someone over who has a wheelchair, measure your doorways and get a ramp. They're $150 on Amazon. It's the law, assholes.

Every single day of shooting, upon leaving the set I would have to have a pleasant, though tense, discussion with the production team.

"I'll be back in twelve hours. Yes, I know, we are falling behind, and yes, I am ruining everything. And I'll be back in twelve hours." It's known as the broken-record technique: maintain a pleasant tone and just say the same thing over and over again. You can do it with your children or on nasty calls from creditors. Just keep repeating what you're able to do until you have to hang up or run away from your phone or they hang up from boredom. Some of the production staff made a point of saying how hard they worked around me: "I'm a sixty-five-year-old Teamster and I only get an eight-hour turnaround and that means, because I live in Riverside, I only get four hours of sleep a night, but I have to drive this huge van all day long."

"Mac, I think what you're intimating is that I'm a pussy. And I am. You're tougher than I am. And your situation sucks and is really dangerous for your health and the health of people sharing the road with you. Instead of getting a ride in your Megavan, I'll take a Lyft home, but I'll be back in twelve hours!"

"The makeup department is the first to be here and the last to leave, and one of the hairstylists has brain cancer AND she's pleasant as hell all day and seventy years old and she can come back in nine hours. She gets here two hours before you and she has BRAIN CANCER."

"Yes, I understand that I am a bad person without moral backbone and that everyone else hopes to die in service of a Netflix comedy. I'll see you in twelve hours."

"Is there ANY way we can work around this? We'll get you an assistant! And overtime! Extra money!"

"Will this assistant sleep FOR me in a *Freaky Friday*, *Back to the Future* time machine thing that you buy with the production money I'm wasting by sleeping? Also, you're already paying me a tremendous amount of money. How much more could 'more' matter if I'm an inadequate robot?" (And though I'm not saying this part out loud, because it seems ungrateful, unprofessional, and beside the point, because I desperately want to be making this TV show: I feel like horse dung, even with a twelve-hour turnaround. As soon as I get home, I pass out and only wake up when the driver honks to pick me up the next day. Yes, I had a driver who had a heart condition. You met Mac earlier in this text and he's a Jewish Trump supporter.)

```
MAC: You have it good.
```

See me nod with direct eye contact? I HEAR THAT, Mac. I know I am a lucky little bitch princess.

And then, it was over. We did it! I don't remember most of it due to being sleepy, but I made it and earned the average cost of a house in Southern California! And everybody else did it! On a ton less sleep than I had! We all made it through the whole season one! Three months of shooting for twelve (12) episodes! And though I know the experience was awesome—or at least the parts that I was semiconscious for were awesome—after rewatching, I think childbirth is the best analogy. After nine months and you finally meet the baby, you think, "Is it mine?" Yes, Ms. Bamford. You're listed as an executive producer. "Oh! I guess I can see it a little now. Around the eyes. Yes! THIS IS MY BEAUTIFUL BABY."

When the show came out, Netflix said, "You have a second season!" I thought, "It's just three months! I can do it again! I'll buy a house that's in a fancy neighborhood (has trees in it)! It will be better this year because everyone knows that I'll do the twelve-hour thing and I know what to expect and it will be easier."

And I got to do a second season! With the same group of insanely wonderful talented professionals!

After the first season, I knew that I was going to need some more help to make it through the nine weeks of shooting. I asked for an on-set tent to escape to (emotionally and physically). It's not Dom Pérignon, a masseuse, and a private baby llama, but it may have seemed that ridiculous to most people on set. In between shots, I had a little pup tent with a cot, a sleeping bag, and a pillow. I offered to buy it all myself, but Netflix covered it. Have you ever been on a med that makes you sleepy? Maybe you can whip yourself up for an hour with coffee, but your head is going to fall drowsily forward during the most exciting of opportunities, and that includes your dream job.

How this worked was: the director would ask to set up the next shot, and while other actors were going over their lines, socializing, being conscious, I would RUN to my little black tent, zip myself in, and wait for the soft tones of "Maria, cameras up" to wake me from a dream of eating my way concentrically through a cinnamon roll. I'd then unzip the tent, RUN back to the stage, "act," and wait for the next time I could fall over like dead wood.

A few times in the beginning of the season, uninformed production or union guys would unzip the tent and say, "Hey, what's in here, man? OH! Sorry," and back away quickly.

I still feel lightly ashamed of this, even though I know it made being half-asleep all day with meds more manageable.

And that season was shot, and again, I'm extremely grateful that I got the once-in-a-lifetime opportunity. But again, I still felt—in my body and brain—like a blobby tennis sock, filled with Blue Bunny strawberry ice cream. A sickening excuse for quality.

When the Great and Powerful Netflix said no to a third season, I was sad but also "whew!"ing with relief. It was a dream, and sometimes the dream is a lot more challenging than you think it's going to be. Turns out my first choice for my career, stand-up comedy, is perfect for me: sixty minutes a day max, twenty-three-hour turnaround.

I hope that a new medication regimen comes along and sweeps me off my feet and once again I am able to produce and perform well for hours like I did pre–mental breakdown. But until that happens, I'll be over here writing myself to sleep.

22. My Tenth Cult: Recovering Couples Anonymous

Scott! My husband! Always mentioned! Not yet explored!

Scott. As I mentioned, we met online and he was on board with my mentals from the get. We went on one OKCupid date for lunch and he seemed interesting. Warm, dry hands! I liked his painting and we knew someone in common. He knew my comedy via his friend Drew. And it wasn't a negative association.

Second date, hike in Griffith Park. Scott, like a floodgate had opened, told me everything about his childhood and his life and every girlfriend he'd ever had and almost every sexual experience he'd ever had, all in a period of about ninety minutes. Some of the stories covered:

- His dad throwing knives at him and his brother
- His dad abusing his mom
- Working with famous artists
- All the girlfriends he is still friends with

After the hike, we went for coffee and he saw someone from the art world and got really anxious and wanted to know whether I thought he should say hello or not.

Today I find this manner of delivery of information adorable. Now I understand why he felt safe and obliged to tell me everything, because, just like me, Scott overshares. He has some very good embellishing skills, but first and foremost he likes to go into extensive detail about what exactly happened even if it might make people uncomfortable. Sounds familiar. We both like to GET IT OUT, NOW.

At the time, however, I was horrified. It was a four-hour date. I got home from the date EXHAUSTED. What WAS that? I agreed in theory to another date, but I wasn't sure. My family was in town for ten days and I thought, "I'd like to take a week to think about this." This is something I had never before done—taken a week or *thought* about dates. He had said he wanted to show me his sketchbook and I love sketches, so I figured, why not? I agreed to meet him at the coffee shop nearest my house so that I could leave toot suite and just tell him later (via text) that I had a feeling that we weren't a good match. Nobody can argue with feelings.

But Scott showed up with totally different energy. He was a happily deflated balloon. The second date had just been that he needed to tell me everything. Scott is like the Warner Brothers frog: when he sings, he sings, but when he's quiet, he is quite happy just ribbeting and making it seem like he never sang at all.

We had coffee, and he showed me his incredible sketchbook with lots of beautiful writing in it and his homemade, inspiring, and autobiographical comic book, and I was totally surprised that I really wanted to see him again.

When we started dating, Scott, well aware of my mentals, would do this fun bit whenever I seemed down. He would say, bashfully smiling into his chest, his eyes looking up with joy, "I'm depressed TOO!" It always makes me laugh. At the time, I didn't take in that he was telling me something about himself while joking despite the fact that I am a comedian and I KNOW THIS. Jokes are always based in truth. If a guy is joking about how much he hates his wife, the odds are pretty good he hates his wife. Just FYI, next time you're hardiharring at the ironic misogyny/racism/rape joke of your favorite emcee, know that they may be a misogynist, racist rapist.

I don't want to speak for Scott, but I know he would be okay with me saying he's got PTSD from a wack childhood. On a bad day, he'll say, "I think I have brain damage. I'm insane." His therapist and psychiatrist have suggested he might have the bipolar, and in our seventh year together, he's upped his Prozac to 60 mg per day—which I'm not sure if that's a good or bad reflection on me, but just to say we are both a bit cray, in a way that works for us.

Our first Christmas, Scott wore this handmade (by me from thrift and puffy paint) sweater that left a rash around his neck the whole evening. I am wearing his thrifted Xmas sweater gift.

Scott loves painting and he loves the people he loves, but the outside world—with the exceptions of music, babies (from a five-foot distance), animals of any kind, and his friends Drew, Ed, Jeff, and Jessica—can sometimes overwhelm him. Like me, Scott—and do not try to approach him—is not classically "charming." I ADORE THIS ABOUT HIM. Because that is what I'm like, not immediately likable. You will KNOW if he likes you, but it could take a while.

Before we met, he would blame his moodiness on circumstance. He worked mostly in construction-type jobs doing faux finishing and gold leaf, or as a ghost painter for famous artists (sometimes working on extremely elaborate drawings and paintings for nine to twelve hours a day). He was in physical pain (arthritis and carpal tunnel), or he had job stress (one contractor would wait months after the job was completed to pay him and would have screaming fits). So by the time we'd been together for three years, many of those stressful elements of his life had been removed. We paid off his student loans and moved to a quiet suburb, and all he had to do was exactly what he'd always wanted: paint full-time. When he realized his dreams, however, his feelings of "insanity" didn't go away. He had the sad realization that "Uh-oh. This is just HOW I FEEL ALL THE TIME."

We were three months into our relationship when we decided we needed a therapist. We were six months in when we attended our first marriage preparatory weekend. We were one year in when we headed to Seattle to learn from THE GOTTMAN INSTITUTE the GOTTMAN METHOD. The Gottman Method was created by a married therapist couple who, through scientific study in their LOVE LAB, say they can predict divorce just by watching a couple over a weekend on camera.

According to their findings, there are six behaviors that predict divorce. One of these is the "harsh start-up." Like instead of saying, "Good morning!" you say, "Fuck me. You still here?"

Their research shows that if your discussion begins with a harsh start-up, it will inevitably end on a negative note. The Gottmans proclaim that 96 percent of the time, you can predict the outcome of a conversation based on the first three minutes of the interaction.

They teach how to avoid the Four Horsemen of the Apocalypse in relationships: criticism ("That's a stupid sailboat"), contempt ("You and your GODDAMNED sailboat"), defensiveness ("What sailboat?"), and stonewalling ([*NO REACTION TO SAILBOAT*]).

We had the extra $1,200 to throw into the abyss—the abyss being a basement convention-center weekend in Seattle. Scott got the flu on the way there and on the first day was visibly ill; the actual Gottmans themselves saw him and told us we should go home. For $1,200, we learned that if one of you is ill, don't show up to a seminar. Your partner is ill, Maria. Stay home. Jesus.

One of the Gottman principles is that couples need to remember the positive, wonderful experiences they've had on the regs. Yes, that is helpful. We have had a TON of good times. But to mythologize a narrative in which we disallow any of the rough experiences would be disrespectful to just how much we've done together. When comics get together, a favorite topic of conversation is Tanking at Shitty Gigs. As a couple, Scott and I have truly Tanked and Hosted/Executive Produced a few memorable Bombs. Much like me and casinos, Scott, myself, and driving under the influence of nitro cold brew do not mix well. Just as in my comedy career, if I orchestrate the right wrong environment, we can set ourselves up for a surprisingly awful time.

Until Scott, the longest relationship I had ever maintained in adulthood was one year. Eight years into our union, HOW DID WE DO IT? HOW ARE WE DOING IT? The answer is that we make each other laugh AND are getting any kind of help we can. As of this writing, we have joined my fifth and Scott's very first twelve-step support group: Recovering Couples Anonymous.

Prior to joining RCA, Scott and I were not doing particularly well. We were in Duluth after my mom's passing, the Covid numbers were still rising, and I was having difficulties with Scott's mood management. One of the great gifts that the twelve-step and self-help movements have given me is the belief—even if it seems deluded—that you can recover! Despite the ill will of others, no discernible market base, and lacking any previous evidence of success: YOU CAN DO IT. I cling to the philosophy of creative visualization and the great mantra "Feel the fear and do it anyway." I say to myself:

I am right now in an extremely safe, fun, joyful, supportive, and productive relationship with my husband, Scott!

Let's go ahead and capitalize on it!

I AM RIGHT NOW IN A SAFE, LOVING, SUPPORTIVE, FUN, INSPIRING RELATIONSHIP WITH MY HUSBAND, SCOTT MARVEL CASSIDY, A GOOFY HANDSOME BEAST!

And what if yelling that sentence in the mirror a few times a day with a smile on my face builds confirmation bias of the positive aspects of our relationship? It certainly can't hurt. Unless I'm doing it at 3 a.m. and waking up Scott (who is a very light sleeper and is terrified by my nightly conversations that he says always err on the side of a speech of righteous indignation).

Here's the issue as far as I see it. You get the genetic, historic, familial traits that you get. Some are awesome, some are awful. Then you bring those traits to another person. Ideally, an almost divine healing takes place that can't happen outside of the context of committed romantic relationships.

I come from a passive-aggressive lineage. I would much rather completely withdraw in the moment from conflict—or from any circumstance in which there is a danger of rejection or hurt—and then complain publicly, but indirectly, later.

Scott comes from a family of four kids. Their parents are now deceased, but their childhood, by most accounts, was a disaster: poverty, physical and emotional violence, sleeping in the woods to escape belt whips to butts for mistakes on homework assignments. Scott has been in therapy off and on for around twenty years. It was his decision to keep his distance from his family, to not try TOO hard to get love because of possible disappointment. For his mood issues, he has self-soothed with food, by banging his head against the wall, or by isolating himself and painting to music.

One problem that we've consistently had is anger management on both sides. When I feel angry, I withdraw, judge the other person as being Eville, shut down, and think of death: not great. (But polite? Ha-ha!) When Scott gets angry, he uses the f-word for almost every word and says things he doesn't mean. Scott yells. I didn't grow up with yelling. He will also throw or slam a thing (not in my direction, but in frustration). He then apologizes within an hour. I'm also good at apologizing—so we've got that going for us.

We've had great stretches of time when this doesn't happen or we're able to use the tools we've both learned to shut it down: taking breaks, turning toward each other with phrases such as "Let's start again," and jokes (the best). But at this moment in time, given the pandemic, the Trump years, and my mom's death, we've hit a new bottom in the Cassidy-Bamford Family. As a result, I asked Scott to go to an anger-management course and I'm going to individual therapy again. In RCA, we're learning more tools for de-escalation. I've read everything: *It Takes One to Tango* by Winnifred M. Reilly, every book by the Gottmans, and I am currently halfway through *Saving Your Marriage Before It Starts* by Les and Leslie Parrott. I will buy a dramatic title from the self-help section of any independent bookstore. I am not shy. Scott has noticed that I'll be reading a book about relationships and as I'm reading, I'll slowly turn my head toward him in dismay.

SCOTT: What? What did I do?

MARIA [*thinking, "Oh God, oh God, oh God! We are doomed!"*]: Nothing, but . . . well, read this!

Or I'll be reading something else and then I give him a twenty-minute back massage and circle scratch because he's wonderful.

SCOTT: Where'd this come from?

MARIA: I love you!

From books, I've learned (and this may sound elementary) it's not good to assume the worst intentions of your partner. For example, if Scott doesn't help me make the bed in the morning because he's already making breakfast, there are two interpretations:

I think, "Scott is making breakfast for himself and the dogs while I make our bed. I know he'd make me breakfast [a Diet Coke and a handful of peanuts] if I asked. MY HUSBAND IS A SCRUMPTIOUS BUNCAKE!"

Or, like an end-time preacher, I can look for the dark side:

"There he is! Making breakfast for himself and the dogs instead of helping me make the bed! I'm a career woman left alone to tuck blankets under a mattress! MY HUSBAND IS A MAN MONSTER—A MAN-STER!"

But Scott agreed to accompany me to Duluth to be there for my mom's care and passing and postmortem processing—for four months. That's a long time in a very small community with my family. Scott has a life and a studio practice and friends and our beloved dogs back in LA. Scott uprooting himself and traveling to Duluth is a HUGE SIGN that he is committed and cares about my well-being. You would assume, given those actions, that I would be totally CONVINCED that he is the Best Husband in the Whole World. Indeed, HE WORE A HANDMADE LION COSTUME I MADE!

But, as we've seen, the vilifying of loved ones is sort of my "zone." I blamed my mother and father and sister for thousands of things and then moved to California to stop being "scapegoated" by their benign presence. I'm aware that anything I experienced was an inconsequential inconvenience along the lines of my mother asking me to wear pantyhose, as opposed to third-degree burns given to you by a cattle brand on purpose by a cult leader in Upstate New York.

But let's get to the most recent low point:

We're in Duluth at the Residence Inn on Central Entrance. My mom is dying, and I'd like to stay in Duluth and be with my family. Scott feels odious. He feels like he has nothing to do, nowhere to go (he's afraid of Covid and terrified of using the car), and that he's totally trapped. Scott has PTSD when he's around my family (due to his real childhood trauma), so his feelings are POWERFUL. I offer helpful solutions like: TAKE THE CAR! DRAW STUFF IN THE WOODS! That is not what he needs. He just needs me to know he feels poorly. I get frustrated. Why can't he just draw and paint anywhere? Yes, it'd be great if he had some sort of studio, but plenty of people don't have studios. There aren't any comedy clubs at the moment and *I'm* doing comedy—even if it's over a table outside with light rain to one person and their confused five-year-old they have brought along. (The five-year-old is very funny and probably should have closed the show.)

I don't have patience for his feelings. I tell him as much. Now—after me judging him outright—he is, rightfully, MAD. MAD AS HELL. And in his style, just as my style is withdrawal and saying absolutely nothing, he says everything, including lots of things with swears. Not necessarily cruel, but true irritations he has with me and my family. It's not the greatest time for that, since, as noted before, my mother is dying, and if I haven't already mentioned it, I LOVE MY FAMILY. The problem, as I see it, is that Scott needs to talk to someone besides me about this. (TALK TO SOMEONE ELSE!) But, like all my ideas at this time, they are not good ideas for him. For the past two days he's slept a lot with his headphones on in our hotel room. That's how he needs to take care of himself. That is not what I would do if I were him. But I am NOT him, and therein lies the difficulty.

After a miserable time for him, Scott leaves Duluth to go home to be with the dogs. He loves the dogs. I know he loves me, but the dogs are his friend-children. I'm starting to feel the reality of being in a mall hotel by myself for a month (which really is nice, with access to a Michaels across a parking lot).

And that is the holding of darkness and light in a relationship for me. I can love someone one moment, be adversarial the next. This applies to everyone. Even you, dear skimmer. By the by, Scott's mood shifted completely once he decided to go home to LA. Relieved, he was now playful and fun and apologetic for being such a dong for the past few days. I ask him to please, next time, bleed off his pissiness to somebody else. CALL ONE OF YOUR SEVERAL PALS, BELOVED SCOTT! I have no pride—please gossip about me to someone else besides me, as I'm an ache in the tuchus, but I can't be the only audience.

Scott and I might not be qualified or able to participate in a Gottman Couples Retreat (a week-long program on an island for which you must be prescreened; I'm not sure if we could make the cut with our dual diagnoses), but we can definitely shell out the sixty-five dollars via PayPal for an online, court-approved, four-hour anger-management course. We wrote a song together ABOUT fighting. We would never be in a *People* magazine foldout of Power Couples, but we might be considered for *bp Magazine*'s Relationships issue that comes out once a year!

Now, fourteen months later, in RCA, we have a sponsor couple, Darlene and John. Romantic partnerships remind me of stand-up comedy. Some people will have a very strong opinion of your creation (the relationship). Everyone is an expert. And maybe the booker is right about your sock puppet with the Filipino accent. But it doesn't matter what they think. It doesn't matter if other people think you and your spouse(s) are the next Barack and Michelle or TLC Sister Wives. You get to love whom and what you love.

I have a housekeeper. Marta is a single mother with strong opinions. I pay Marta fifty-five dollars an hour. She drives a late-model Lexus SUV and owns her home outright in Southern California. All four of her kids have gone to college. I drive a six-year-old Toyota RAV4 that a rat has moved into and eaten the wiring. Marta and I were chatting recently in my limited Spanish, and she asked how long Scott and I had been married. I said six years. She said in Spanish, "I wasn't sure about him in the beginning. I was worried it wasn't going to last, but then you stayed together. And you've gained weight [*pointing at my belly*] and seem happier." Marta, I can read shade in a second language. You got that right, Marta, it's amazing we made it this far. And I have put on five pounds!

I felt distraught after Marta said that—that somehow she doubted my choice of partner or our choice of each other in the beginning and that it sounds like she's been sitting on that info for a while. But I need to remind myself: How do *I* feel about my relationship and Scott? Right now, in this moment, great! We're working our second step in RCA, and we get to make a culty higher-power collage with Darlene and John (who Zoom with us once a week and we get to see their poodle).

A fellow comic friend of mine got an email from a stranger that said something like, "YOU'RE NOT SKILLED AT WHAT YOU DO! LET ME HELP! I'm GREAT and I think together we can make you BETTER!" That isn't constructive criticism, that's a salesman. Anyone who says—about something you've developed in your life (creatively or personally)—"THE WHOLE THING IS WRONG! LET'S BURN IT TO THE GROUND AND START OVER!" is a bag of dried fish heads (they stink). Metaphorically, I like a chair that's been spray-painted a few times over the years. Let's take exactly what we have and try to make tiny improvements. Let's not get back to bare bones and find out that we've lost so much weight our organs are going to shut down.

Scott and I have both fought for what we have—which (and I'll let him speak for himself) in my mind is a very loving, fairly moody monogamous romantic relationship that works for us. It may not be what anyone else wants—you and your perfect easygoing sex romp of fifty years—but we have lots of laughs and pizza parties and get it on about once a week, and that's more than enough for me.

LOVE FESTIVAL, BY SCOTT MARVEL CASSIDY

1. Lie down on your kitchen floor.
2. Communicate in some way that it's time for a love festival. For example: "IT'S TIME FOR A LOVE FESTIVAL!"
3. Have your spouse and pets, or whomever you feel love for, sit on your chest while you give them belly rubs.
4. Remind them, "It's a love festival and the only ticket is a smile!"
5. Repeat as needed.

23. Obligatory Suicide Disclaimer 

FIFTH-GRADE FEELS—CRAYON GOTH

Saying "Hang in there" to someone who has experienced months or decades of mental illness with no end in sight is the height of cruelty. I am not encouraging you (sexily?) or anyone else to (glamorously?) kill themselves. But I have total empathy for those who do. I have friends and family members who have died by suicide, and who were heroes for holding on as long as they did with unimaginable suffering.

"It gets better" is a slogan that some in the mental health world have borrowed from the LGBTQ+ movement. Hopefully, it does get better. But it doesn't always. For me, a very, very pretty fifty-two-YO cis-lady person with bipolar II (BP lite) and full health coverage, I felt better with meds (and monumentally better the first two days OFF MEDS—AMIRITE?). I also have online therapy, various twelve-step-group memberships, and a life in sunny Southern California, where the culture is such that if you tell strangers about your current emotional state, they will usually respond with, "Amazing!" I've had three hospital stays and three rounds of outpatient treatment, and my insurance paid for all of it, except for once when I had to give them cash up front, but that was my bad because I was too mental to call the facility beforehand to make sure they took my Blue Cross.

I'd hope everyone is willing to ride out a resurgence of the illness the eightieth time, but I know I didn't feel like I had it in me when I was ill. To the friends and family members of people who experience suicidal thoughts or have attempted suicide: Maybe don't, uh, admonish them? Like, "Hey, you, never do that again, you got that, you Dummie™?" It's an illness. People sometimes die of it. It's nobody's fault. (It's also not a #blessing—they weren't destined for another, better world, you spiritual cuntwagons.) And yes, I'm talking to you, shamanic homeopathic-crystal fans. Stardust Thunderbolt, you live in Ojai, I get it. You don't yet know that breast cancer can return. You've saged, magnetized your pain-body, and soaked in a tub of fairy pomade. And yet breast cancer can come back like a motherfucker. My mom got holy hands held, oiling drum ceremonies, she abstained from sugar and white flour for two years straight. And then she died. Yes, Freeway Bougainvillea, you, too, can die. We all die. Even if we do a six-week Tapatío cleanse and swim to work.

Like most people, I've thought of suicide between eight and ninety times per day since around the age of nine. At forty, I gathered a bunch of pills from all the new prescriptions I'd been given over the years and thought about it seriously, but I never took them. I went to the hospital instead. Even regarding suicide, I'm not a can-do person. But I can't promise anyone that if I got sick again that I wouldn't kill myself, because mental-illness episodes BLOW with ALL THE CAPS.

This is not a published cry for help. I'm on a good mix of Supa-Sweet™ meds, have lots of support from friends, family, pets, and a loving hub. But I want to give props of love to people who have attempted or died by suicide. Again, with suicide, I've always been more of an armchair quarterback than a player on the field, but here's my Hail Mary pass to anyone who's thinking of offing themselves:

That therapist-prescribed voice-mail message of "Hang up and dial 911" is the worst. And if you have a non-white skin color or have any antisocial behaviors, it might get you killed. At the very least, 911 can be useless, traumatic, and expensive. A better option is an emergency mobile mental health response team—which, if you google those words plus your zip, might be available in your area and are good numbers to have at the ready. I've called 911 and gotten help, but I know that's a privilege—use your own feels. If you can go for help at a hospital with an advocate, someone looking out for you, so you aren't all of a sudden fucked, that, of course, is ideal. I've driven and hung out with a few friends for psychiatric emergencies. It was fun for me. I got sandwiches. That said, if NONE OF THESE ARE AVAILABLE TO YOU:

LOWER THE BAR! GET ANY KIND OF SHITTY-ASS HELP. And let's acknowledge that getting shitty-ass mental health help is NOT EASY. Do not be tricked by the crafty-inkwell-script, barnyard-wedding messages on mental health organization websites that declare, "Ask for help!" or, "HEY you! Tell someone!" or by the new flood of Mental Health Awareness Day memes from Kaiser Permanente (who last I heard might have had its therapists striking because of reportedly not allowing patients more than one visit every three months, even in cases of brutal trauma and debilitating diagnosis). During "peak surge" hours, the national suicide hotline, 800-273-8255, sometimes has a forty-five- to ninety-minute wait. But, right now, while writing, I just tried texting and got a counselor in five minutes and it's a weekend! Parts of our society function! Try dialing the new one: 988!

BUT IF THAT FAILS: Call AT&T! Call Domino's! Call an anti-abortion "clinic"! See if they're pro-life for your life. All of their literature says, "Life is a gift." Have someone who answers their phone prove it to you. Yes, none of these are good and could be crap. But you deserve that free, shitty-ass crap help. I have, in times of distress, called small businesses in my neighborhood. I once got a Hertz rental car associate to say, "I guess I believe every human life has value," before she hung up on me. See what you can get from a gas-station attendant. Your local coffee-shop employee, if not already in tears from a khaki-panted haircut yelling at her for not making a triple-shot cap with skim milk, might have a David Bowie tattoo to compliment, and for the simple glory of being asked for their opinion, your barista might share a handful of their CBD popcorn. Call out, publicly, in a place where you feel safe, like a used-book store, "ANYBODY! QUICKLY NOW! GIVE ME A REASON TO GO FORWARD!"

If fast food is your comfort zone, go walking from SUV to SUV—conduct an open-source Burger King drive-thru tally of whether life is worth living. If you're in a mixed state of mania and depression, it might be something you'd excel at. Religious institutions and cults—if you ignore talk of Satan and high membership fees—are great resources in a pinch. Tunelessly wail "Somewhere Over the Rainbow" in the closest church until someone invites you to accept Christ as your personal savior and you get down to the business of getting some ears on your story. Get into Scientology for one month full bore and on day thirty, PULL OUT, for a joyful bump of escape velocity!

Visit your local junior high school receptionist's desk and ask to go to the nurses' office. Tweet at me (@mariabamfoo) nonstop with links to your YouTube channel. If I am not asleep or staring menacingly into a *Retirement for Dummies* book, I will "like" every post. I support you! From a great distance! Which is the definition of free, shitty-ass help!

But seriously, let's get corporate America on your depression, stat. Treat yourself right and call the front desk of a Hilton property (Hilton Pasadena 626-577-1000). I bet the concierge at the Ritz-Carlton Orlando (407-246-2400) has a loving affect. Dial 0, call 411, go to a nail salon at a strip mall, sit down on one of those thrones, put your feet in the tub, and start articulating your inner life into the noxious fumes. I'm at a Coffee Bean & Tea Leaf right now, and a man experiencing what looks like schizophrenia as well as houselessness got a few kind words from the manager before he was asked to leave. I bought him lunch. Again, not a solution, but it is better than nothing at all. This poor man has now settled outside the window, out of the hot sun with his beltless pants all the way down, but he is richer one sandwich and a bottle of Dasani.

If you are truly out of ideas, get to the ER. As you probably already know, the quality of care can be anywhere from okay to downright horrible. BRING A PAL FOR THIS SCARY ADVENTURE. During the quarantine, I drove a friend with psychosis to a psych-only ER in LA (outpatient only). The waiting area had a big-screen TV playing

CNN. Therefore, the TV was replaying—in between commercials for walk-in tubs—video of George Floyd being murdered, over and over and over again for the two hours we were sitting there. My friend is Black. There were several other people in the ER who were also living, breathing human beings of various shades. And the emergency psych clinic's only offering in the waiting room was repetitive play-by-play footage of an unarmed man being suffocated to death by law enforcement. We finally (after an overworked mental health worker had a minute) got the TV channel changed to the Cartoon Network, which, thankfully, was not A LIVE-ACTION SNUFF FILM. And my friend did get meds and an appointment with a doctor for the next day. THIS WAS THE WORST AND MAXIMUM SHITTY-ASS HELP THEY COULD HAVE RECEIVED. And my friend is still alive.

As far as financial backlash, I've been saddled with extensive medical debt and had collection agencies calling me all the time and threatening by letter that they are "NOW TAKING LEGAL ACTION." And I am also now alive, and I paid that debt off over a period of eight years at a rate of sometimes two dollars a month.

Please don't hurt yourself or anyone else. Do something else instead. Even if it's harmful! Suicide is a one-off. You can do meth at least twice without consequences! (I don't know if that's true.) Knock yourself out with a forty-ounce keg of Baileys Irish Cream and a Dairy Queen Blizzard. You do not want to miss any additions to the Dairy Queen product line! Did you know they have a FUDGE-STUFFED COOKIE now? Postmate that mess while you wait for the response team (your friend Tookie). If you cannot access these luxuries, go to the pantry. Get a jar of Skippy equivalent and finish it IN HOUSE while asking a volunteer to stand on your lower back. And use this time to try things you never thought you'd do: basic training, plural marriage, improv street comedy.

I'm not always trying to keep myself from cutting my own throat *Deadwood* style, but mental illness isn't always preventable. There's a powerlessness that takes hold, as in any other disease—a sense that when you get sick, you might not make it. When this happens, you may not remember that there is an official document in your junk drawer that you've signed promising everyone not to kill yourself. The unfathomable anguish in your brain is begging you 24-7 to immediately stop the madness. I'm saying this because I don't want to get down on myself if I do it. Which would be humorous. As I couldn't get mad at myself anymore! I'd be dead. Ha-ha.

I have a friend named Mike who has attempted suicide several times due to major depressive disorder. He's been told that his mentals are "treatment-resistant," which sounds a lot like "noncompliant" heart disease or "won't play ball" multiple sclerosis. My pal has done everything to get help. He's been on every med, had electroconvulsive therapy tens of times, gotten DBS—deep brain stimulation, where they insert tiny electrodes in your head. For years, he had a ticking noise coming from his collarbone that was supposedly tickling his serotonin levels, but he said it did nothing but make him sound like a metronome. He moved to the beach for whatever the ocean is supposed to be good for. He built a sweat lodge. He goes to all the twelve-step programs. He's married to a kind person. He's a pet papa and a skilled artist, and he volunteers in his community. And in the twenty years I've known him, he has made almost biennial suicide attempts that have only been caught by his spouse at the last minute. And I don't think it's because he hasn't been asked by Byron Katie the Four Questions That Can Change Your Life. It's because his brain is built to feel appalling. If I told him, "Hey, girl, it gets better," not only would I be rude for not recognizing Mike's preferred pronoun, but I'd again be putting the onus of responsibility on him to cure himself.

Scott's grandmother lived to be a hundred and smoked and ate banana splits every day. At sixty, I'd love to start smoking and adopt kids in their thirties who ask me occasionally for twenty bucks and a stiff hug. But if I or anyone else dies of suicide because of whatevs haunted house is in their head, I just want to celebrate that I or you or anyone else was out there crushing and grinding for as long as we could.

BREAKFAST

Serves one.

"Existence is intolerable. Cooking shouldn't have to be!"

1. Take a jar of peanut butter (I prefer super-chunky salted Jif). If you like, pre-chill in the fridge or on a window ledge.
2. Open the jar lid by pounding it on the ground or a countertop, or by taking a hammer to it.
3. Plunge a fork or spoon deeply into the jar until there is a three- to four-inch-high hillock of PB atop it.

Variation: For an even quicker morning ritual, keep the lid OFF and raw-dog it with your index finger.

Thank you for reading. I hope you are doing super great.

APPENDIX

I've always wanted to rewrite the Koran, but I still have to read it. Until then, I give you Maria Bamford's twelve-step program for Dumb Bees™.

THE TWELVE (Silly) STEPS OF (Super Stupid) TWELVE-STEP PROGRAMS (My Version—Which Is Unapproved and Apostate)

1. **We admitted we were powerless over [parking illegally/chicken strips/Natty Light/pirating cable]—and that our lives had become unmanageable.**

For the purposes of working the steps on something you might relate to, let's admit we are powerless over parking illegally. It is my current problem. I just did it yesterday. I parked in a red zone while my friend said, "You're in the red zone." I am powerless over parking illegally. Despite a friend shaming me, despite the financial retribution of a ticket, I will not stop.

Powerless is in the grips of the weightlifter—if you can't handle it, it qualifies! Unmanageable, same thing. Feel like your food-pantry-volunteering obsession is taking time away from your kids? Sounds like your helping others get tuna has gone beyond normal usage!

As far as my twelve-step attendance has addressed, I have been "powerless" (despite trying to change/not being able to change at all) over the following behaviors:

- (1980–90) Dieting/binging/purging (joined OA in 1990)
- (1990–94) Medical debt/not being able to support myself financially/borrowing money (joined DA in 1994)
- (1989–2004) One-night stands with strangers/dating guys who were not that into me (joined SLAA in 2004)
- (2020–21) Scott's and my regulating of conflict (joined RCA in 2020)

2. **We came to believe that a power greater than ourselves could restore us to sanity.**

I can pay for parking. For that reason alone, I'm lightly insane to continue parking illegally. I also, as an underemployed comedian, have PLENTY OF TIME TO LOOK FOR LEGAL PARKING. Currently, I don't NEED to park illegally.

3. **We made a decision to turn our will and our lives over to the care of God as we understood Him.**

If you take the ominous Catholic bejeezus out of it, this is just saying out loud that maybe I'll be open to hear a few other ideas besides my own. When I think of how this might work with my criminal parking addiction, maybe I could call someone whenever I'm about to park illegally. It might not stop me, but it might provide an element of harm reduction, in that I'd be more aware of what I'm doing, or at the very least have a giggle. Maybe the person on the other end of the phone would have some ideas better than my own or stop me from doing what I've done before (for example, now I call someone before I agree for the hundredth time to a show in an outdoor burrito restaurant in the Fairfax district, sixty minutes from my house). Because if I tell my friend Robin my plans, she might remind me, "Hey, don't you hate outdoor shows at 10 p.m.? Don't you always LIKE to get out of them and then feel bad about it for days afterward?"

```
ME: Oh, right! But THIS TIME IT WILL BE DIFFER-
    ENT. And they ASKED me. I feel special and
    alive being wanted!
ROBIN: Okay! Well, have a great time!
```

I will call Robin later, having done exactly what I've always done—said yes to a geographically challenging locale and then bailed unprofessionally—and Robin will not be surprised. Yes, I still might do the dysfunctional pattern, but I'll have done things SLIGHTLY differently by getting my friend Robin involved!

4. **We made a searching and fearless moral inventory of ourselves.**

WORKSHEETS! My favorite!

This gets people in the weeds—to me, it's oddly fun, but I'll put it in tiny font, so skip if tiresome.

This is where some twelve-steppers get saintly, making tons of graphs that help them assess their minuscule "character defects." For me, I just think of this as a list of what I do that's bumming me out, what I wish I could stop doing and can't, how it's affected other people, and what I might do to replace it.

Let's work step four on PARKING ILLEGALLY:

FEAR

That I'll be late and there's not enough time and I won't have the right money for a parking lot and then I'll be even later, and people will be mad at me and I'm a failure anyway because I'm late.

MY PART

Entitlement: Feeling like I shouldn't have to follow rules of society that everyone follows because I'm either too big a deal or a miscreant who doesn't matter, no one can even see my three-thousand-pound vehicle in front of the fire hydrant.

Love of excitement: The thrill of not knowing whether I'll have to pay the equivalent of a round-trip airline ticket for a parking spot or even GET TOWED TO GLENDALE! (I have been towed to Glendale.)

Fear of intimacy with the moment: I don't like being early because that means more time, alone, by myself, sitting with no podcasts or soundtracks. I don't want to have any boredom or thoughts or feelings or really the experience of being alive.

Sloth: Not wanting to make any effort.

POSSIBLE "AMENDS" (CULT WORD!)

Do something a little different—JUST FOR TODAY (cult phrase). JFT, allow yourself to be late instead of parking illegally. Or get there really early AND let yourself park illegally while crowing, "Time keeps on slippin'. . . ." Or get there right on time and park legally and reward yourself by going over the speed limit in a school zone. Mix it up. It really doesn't matter—the thing is to change a little tiny bit. Example: Do a heroin eight-ball with a clean needle AND a glass of OJ. It's about harm reduction, not sudden withdrawal.

POSSIBLE REWARDS FOR CHANGING

I might feel sort of proud of myself, more a respectful part of society, less lonely, as I'm acting as a thoughtful member of the world who cares about other people and all the work that has been put in to make my city safe and pleasant to live in.

5. We admitted to God, to ourselves, and to another human being the exact nature of our wrongs.

I guess I'm doing a fifth step now by telling you readers about my parking behaviors. If we were here together, maybe you'd share how you ran over a skateboarder while checking your emails. TEARS AND KNOWING LAUGHS! We are AWFUL LITTLE PIGGIES (and maybe we can change together?).

6. **We're entirely ready to have God remove all these defects of character.**

This is the part in intervention where the mother with a wine problem says, "Yes, this time. This time, I really want help. I'm going to be the best mother to my kids and start a business faux-finishing lake rocks!" It's also a reminder that you PROBABLY ARE NOT READY to stop doing what you're doing.

7. **We humbly asked Him to remove our shortcomings.**

Zoinks. That smells Xtian. HOWEVZ, there *is* something about the psychology of compartmentalization where if I put a problem aside even for a few hours, that can help. (As far as a God removing negative character traits, it seems my bad habit of parking illegally is more powerful than any deity.)

8. **We made a list of all persons we had harmed and became willing to make amends to them all.**

So, for my "party parking," here are the victims of my crimes:

- People of the city of Los Angeles.
- The big, beautiful bus and bus driver.
- Bus riders—people who don't have the luxury of a private vehicle.
- People losing business, time, energy, and trust in society.
- Myself (?). This is questionable, but LA twelve-steppers almost always list "yourself" as a person harmed. That's why you see so many single adults standing in sound baths with cat ears on as an amends to their inner child.

- Let me know at ariamaamfordba@gmail.com! You're now my Parking Sponsor! Thank you for your service!

9. **We made direct amends to such people wherever possible, except when to do so would injure them or others.**

Shut up, leave whomever you hurt alone, and start changing your behavior. Re: parking. I don't think I can do it. I really don't. But that's where telling *you* comes in. Maybe now that I've told you I do it, that will get me to not do it even if it's just for this one day? I haven't done it yet, so if I make it till bedtime, I'll have one day CLEAN.

10. **We continued to take personal inventory and when we were wrong promptly admitted it.**

Whoa, boy. This could be interpreted as an OCD scrupulosity NIGHTMARE, where you're hyperventilating "AM I WRONG?" into a paper bag.

As far as parking, my living amends would be, one second at a time, to change my behavior. I would park in legally designated parking spots that I have paid for.

11. **We sought through prayer and meditation to improve our conscious contact with God as we understood Him, praying only for knowledge of His will for us and the power to carry that out.**

I translate this as "keep talking to people who are trying to do positive things in their lives"—whether that's in twelve-step groups or with friends, my community, or a family reunion in an Embassy Suites hot tub.

12. Having had a spiritual awakening as the result of these steps, we tried to carry this message to illegal parkers, and to practice these principles in all our affairs.

What is "working the steps"? Well, what is *World of Warcraft* or Apples to Apples? It's a reason to meet up with people whom you chat with and who will probably have some influence over your choices. Hopefully, you're becoming the best person you can be (which is an arbitrary value decided by the group). I love the hobby of "personal growth," which I understand some people find to be as meaningful as American Girl doll collecting, but it gives me some shape and meaning to my life. I don't think it's "better" than fly-fishing; it's just what I like. In practice, it's me answering questions about my beliefs and behaviors, looking for patterns in my life (like illegal parking [or procrastination or compulsive whale-watching]) that create chaos and what I might replace them with.

ACKNOWLEDGMENTS

It turns out writing a book requires a lot of effort and support no matter what its quality.

So here is a list of all of the blameless people who have assisted me in this endeavor but who are in no way responsible for its outcome. A thank-you to all, combined with sincere apologies.

Marilyn and Joel Bamford, who made my life possible and encouraged me beyond the point of rationality. I miss you both dearly every moment of every day.

Jackie Kashian, mentor and friend and comedian.

Marketa Velehradska, mentor and friend and therapist.

Solange Castro, mentor and friend and comedian.

Sarah Seidelmann, sister and author/artist/shaman, and loving family of Mark, George, Katherine, Josephine, and Charlie.

Mark Salzman, Jessica Yu, and Ava and Esme Yu-Salzman, beloved friends.

Scott Marvel Cassidy, husband and scrumptious buncake.

Amy O'Connell, friend and Life Genius, pug champion, as well as the Society of the Spectacle eyeglass and emergency mental health center transportation.

The WellRock Gym of Altadena and Jesse and Sarah Holguin, healthcare front line.

Glendale Adventist Medical Center psychiatric staff.

Jeremy, Debbie, Donald, and Stephen Kaplan of Read Books, Eagle Rock, California.

Jess Guinivan, publicist/writer.

Melanie Vesey, comedian and social media guru.

Melinda Hill, Ivana Shein, Robin Reiser, and Liz Glazer, the comedy text feed brain trust

Café de Leche Altadena and Highland Park, owners Anja and Matt Schodorf.

My manager of many lovely years, Bruce Smith.

My booking agent of many lovely years, T. J. Markwalter.

Steve Young and Gary Peterson, mentors, friends, and comedians.

All of these publishing professionals—Jennifer Bergstrom, Aimée Bell, Rebecca Strobel, Sally Marvin, Lucy Nalen, Bianca Ducasse, Lisa Litwack, John Vairo, Karyn Marcus, Kim Laws, Kathryn Kenney-Peterson, Caroline Pallotta, Brigid Black, and Jamie Selzer—who made this book make sense. Thank you respectfully for your mindful patience, of which I have none. You are good people.

The millions of weirdos in twelve-step programs whom I delight in.

Endless names of people who have been kind to me for no reason except to be kind.

The Comedy Community of Los Angeles.

The International OCD Foundation.

The Los Angeles Downtown Women's Center.

The 988 Suicide & Crisis Lifeline.

The Screen Actors Guild, which has provided me with mental health care for the past twenty-five years.

The unbelievably talented and hardworking staff of *Lady Dynamite*, seasons one and two.

Gracious creative sherpas: Dana Gould, Patton Oswalt, Judd Apatow, Mitch Hurwitz, Stephen Colbert, Peter Hannan, Sara Corbett, Leslie Ball, and Frank Conniff, who are generous boosters of my work. And to be honest, I owe them a percentage of my earnings to this day.

ABOUT THE AUTHOR

Maria Bamford was awarded Best Club Comic at the American Comedy Awards and Breakout Comedy Star at Just for Laughs. Her critically acclaimed work includes her web series *The Maria Bamford Show* (featured at the Museum of Modern Art, New York) and *Ask My Mom* (recommended by the *New Yorker*), and her Netflix series, *Lady Dynamite.* Maria's writing has been featured in the *New York Times, LA Weekly,* and the *Onion.* Maria has contributed comedic voice-overs for such animations as Netflix's *Big Mouth* and *BoJack Horseman*; Cartoon Network's *Adventure Time*; PBS's Emmy-winning series *WordGirl*; Nickelodeon's *Kung Fu Panda* and *The Legend of Korra*; and the international hit *Talking Tom & Friends.* She can do about eleven voices, not including her own, but just a little higher and faster. For her mental health advocacy, she's been presented with the International OCD Foundation's Illumination Award and featured at the Psychotherapy Networker Symposium, the Chautauqua Institution, and the Saks Institute for Mental Health Law, Policy, and Ethics Symposium. She's not always right for these rooms, but she's on time and pleasant. *(From MARIA: This was all in the third person, though I wrote it myself, which is slightly creepy. My apologies. If you need help, dial 988. I know. Health care can be super shitty. Go get yourself that shitty-ass help! I love you.)*